"*Pub Theology* is a wonderful, whimsical, and wise story about what happens when a pastor with more questions than answers goes to the pub instead of church."

—John Suk,
author of *Not Sure: A Pastor's Journey from Faith to Doubt*
and former editor of *The Banner*

"This is a book about God's freedom and ours! Bryan Berghoef invites us to pull up a chair and dares us to converse about what matters. No fear! This engrossing and transformative story about how to live an open Christian life will save, stir, and strengthen the faith of many."

—Samir Selmanovic,
author of *It's Really All About God: How Islam, Atheism,
and Judaism Made Me a Better Christian*

Pub Theology

Pub Theology

Beer, Conversation, and God

Bryan Berghoef

CASCADE *Books* · Eugene, Oregon

PUB THEOLOGY
Beer, Conversation, and God

Cascade Books
An Imprint of Wipf and Stock Publishers
199 W. 8th Ave., Suite 3
Eugene, OR 97401

www.wipfandstock.com

ISBN 13: 978-1-61097-422-6

Scriptures taken from the Holy Bible, New International Version®, NIV®. Copyright © 1973, 1978, 1984, 2011 by Biblica, Inc.™ Used by permission of Zondervan. All rights reserved worldwide. www.zondervan.com. The "NIV" and "New International Version" are trademarks registered in the United States Patent and Trademark Office by Biblica, Inc.™

Cataloging-in-Publication data:

Berghoef, Bryan.

   Pub theology : beer, conversation, and God / Bryan Berghoef.

   xvi + 144 p. ; 23 cm. —Includes bibliographical references.

   ISBN 13: 978-1-61097-422-6

   1. Dialogue—Religious aspects. 2. Non-institutional churches. 3. Christianity—Essence, genius, nature. I. Title.

BL410 .B465 2012

Manufactured in the U.S.A.

To Christy

Stranger,
if you passing
meet me and desire to speak to me,
why should you not speak to me?
And why should I not speak to you?

— Walt Whitman, Inscription to *Leaves of Grass,* 1860

Contents

Acknowledgments ix
Introduction xi

1 Before the Pub 1
2 Setting the Table 7
3 Opening Night 12
4 A Story of Two Tables 18
5 The Art of Listening 25
6 An (Un)Safe Place 35
7 Unfiltered 42
8 The Bible Over a Beer 50
9 No Doubt 61
10 Found and Lost 73
11 The Power of Posture 79
12 A Communal Pursuit 87
13 Slippery Slopes, Sailboats, and Safety Nets 98
14 An Evolving Faith 110
15 Tapping into Theology 122
16 Last Call 131

Recommended Reading 139
Bibliography 141

Acknowledgments

This book would not have happened without the help and encouragement of many people. To my fellow Pub Theologians—you know who you are—it is truly a gift to sit down with you each week and dialogue about things that really matter.

Thanks to the crew at Right Brain Brewery (past and present), who not only brew the best beer in town, but have provided such a welcoming space in which to gather. To you, we lift a pint.

To Church on the Corner, London, England. Thanks for articulating a fresh approach to an old idea. And for sharing it.

Thanks to Phyllis Tickle, who reviewed an early draft of this proposal, and whose encouragements and critiques were indispensable.

To Pete Rollins, for inviting a few of us to his hometown of Belfast for a weekend of true theological exploration, and for continuing to push the theological envelope. Keep up the good work.

Many thanks to those who read the manuscript at various stages, providing encouragement and much needed feedback: Mark Hoffmann, Angela Josephine, Chris Lubbers, and my wife, Christy—your feedback and encouragement was crucial! Thanks to Chris for helping make the language as clear as possible. Thanks also to David Ramage, Steve Ruble and Mark and Chris for being willing to sit down and talk about the ins and outs of this enterprise (and the what-have-you's).

Thanks to Christian, Charlie, Rodney, and the folks at Wipf and Stock for believing in this project and helping see it through.

Thanks to my parents, who started me on the journey of faith so long ago. We may not always agree, but you have taught me much about God, for which I am forever grateful.

I wish to thank the community of Watershed for allowing me the space and freedom to pursue the depth and breadth of God outside of the normal channels, and for being an open, accepting community, willing to be challenged, and certainly willing to challenge me. It has been a privilege to be on the journey together.

Finally to my wife, Christy, who has pushed me to write from the start. Your belief in me has been pivotal. I am so grateful for a partner whose wisdom and insights often exceed my own, whose own ability to articulate matters of faith and of the heart are such a blessing and encouragement to me. As I hang out at the pub each week, she attends to the undoubtedly higher calling of getting the kids to bed. I love you, honey. This would not be possible without you.

NOTE: A portion of Chapter 9 originally appeared in the article: "What Does Knowing God Mean?" Traverse City Record-Eagle, Nov 7, 2009.

Introduction

A minister, an atheist, and a few other people walk into a bar . . . The minister says, "Drinking is against God's will for your life." The atheist responds: "He forgot to tell that to Jesus." The others say, "This sounds like a great conversation—can we join?" And so it begins . . .

Most of us like to think of ourselves as being fairly open, fairly welcoming, fairly decent human beings. We'd help anyone in need. We'd be a patient listener if someone had something to say to us. We'd like all people in the world to get along better, and we think that if there were more people like us, that'd be the case. We may have our own convictions and beliefs about the world, about God, about political issues, but in the end—we're a part of the same human family. And for those of us who consider ourselves Christians, we especially feel compelled to act in ways Jesus acted—loving, caring for the marginalized, seeking peace, bringing healing. So if all of the above is true, how do we still account for all the *crap* that goes down in our world?

It seems to me that much of the distress in our world is driven by fear. Fear of what is different. Fear of "the other": other religious views, other sexual orientations, other political views, other ways of being in the world. And these are no longer simply perspectives we read about in books or hear about on television. They are held by our neighbors, our co-workers, perhaps even our friends, those we know personally as well as our virtual "friends." These perspectives are also held by those we may never meet. Yet even these strangers are closer to us than ever in our constantly shrinking world. Someone thinks differently. So what? Well, unfortunately we often don't like this—it threatens us. Especially regarding deeply held views of the world. Too often we react to these different ways of thinking with fear. And fear doesn't stay buried within us. It comes out. We get louder with our message, we withdraw ourselves from the culture to our own safe little enclaves. We toss grenades of "truth" over the wall, hoping to cause more damage than true positive change.

We like to think we are fairly open people, but our actions betray us. There's a disconnect between our perception of ourselves and reality. We've created fictional and virtual selves who always "do the right thing," but when the rubber hits the road in the real world, we often find we're not as open as we like to think.

A recent incident reminded me of this. I received a phone call from a pastor. He leads a growing evangelical church in our area, and I admire the work he is doing. It is a church I have always thought of as one of the more open and progressive churches in our area. I don't speak with him often, so it was nice to hear from him.

"Hi, Bryan."

"Hi, Alex. Nice to hear from you. What's up?" (*Name changed to protect the innocent.*)

"I'm calling about this interfaith prayer gathering that you're a part of."

"Yeah—it's gonna be pretty cool."

"Actually that's what I wanted to talk to you about. I'm not sure that it is. In fact, I have serious concerns about your involvement in this."

"OK . . . What's up?"

"Well, for one thing, it's labeled an "interfaith or no faith" prayer gathering. How can you pray with people who have no faith? How absurd is that? They don't even want to pray!"

"Well, it will also be a space for meditation, silence, and sharing concerns."

"Secondly, I see there is a Wiccan priest involved in this endeavor. A Wiccan! Are you kidding? What kind of people are you associating with? I just think you need to seriously reconsider what kind of a message you're sending by associating with people like this."

"Well, he's actually a really nice guy."

"And how can you even pray with people who don't believe the same way you do? What is even the point of it?"

"OK, Alex. I appreciate your concerns. I think the point of it is acknowledging the common humanity we all have, and giving respect to people who may think differently than I do. It is a space where I can pray according to my tradition, and others can pray according to theirs. Your concern is noted. I do appreciate you thinking of me and getting in touch. But I think this is an important event."

"Well, Bryan, I'd really encourage you to think twice about your involvement in this."

The gathering in question was a "Tax Day Interfaith or No Faith Prayer Breakfast," sponsored by ACORD, the Area Council on Religious Diversity, a local interfaith organization that I am involved in. The meeting was envisioned as an opportunity to gather leaders and people of various faith traditions in our community who have common concerns for how our local and national leaders use our tax dollars to come together and voice those shared concerns in a positive atmosphere of prayer and meditation. A pretty positive event, right? One that could create important bridges of communication in our community among people of varying religious traditions, not to mention the atheists, agnostics, and skeptics among us.

Not everyone felt that way, apparently. This evangelical pastor could not comprehend a space where Christians and those of other faiths or even those without faith could gather and pray and meditate together toward a common end. This is a vivid picture of the crisis of the continuing imperialist (colonialist) attitude of Western evangelicalism. *We* are the ones who own the spiritual real estate, *we* are the ones who are allowed to pray, and unless you submit to doing it on *our* terms, you are not allowed to speak.

"How can you pray with people who don't believe the same way you do? What is even the point of it?" Well, the point is recognizing and respecting the various religious views that people hold in the communities we live in. The point is acknowledging and respecting the beliefs and practices of our neighbors. The point is creating space for the expression of all religious views—even ones that may differ from our own. If this was the response I got from someone I perceived as fairly open and progressive—I could imagine the things others might be saying.

So what does all this have to do with a pub, or theology, for that matter? I thought you'd never ask. My argument in this book is simple: good things happen when we sit down at the same table together and talk honestly about things that matter—and frankly, having a beer doesn't hurt. We don't need to agree on whatever it is that we discuss— that isn't even the point. The point is that we are all stuck here together on this planet (for the unforeseeable future), and we might as well get to know each other while we're here. My sense is that more and more people are hungry for this. People of all backgrounds are opening up about the broadness and diversity of thought and belief around them. And I sense that there is a growing desire for this among my fellow Christians as well. People are ready. Ready to see openness happen in their own lives and communities. Ready to move beyond fear to understanding. Ready to take a brave step forward in learning to live out their own faith honestly and with integrity in the increasingly pluralistic and global world we find ourselves in.

Here's the good news. It's happening. In conversation. At the pub. Over beer. From London to New York to Ann Arbor, people are gathering to communicate, connect, and learn from one another over the topic of religion and theology, of all things.

"Religion? Theology?" you ask. "Who cares about theology any- more? This isn't the 1600s." Turns out lots of people do care. Theology breaks down to "theos," God, and "logos," words. Words about God. Some have said God is dead. Maybe so. Maybe not. But in any case, we're not done talking about him just yet. In fact, it turns out that even the most ardent *a*theists have something to say on the topic. And perhaps, just perhaps, even he—God himself (or herself)—has more to say. He pops up in movies, books (!), the news—even in our own neighborhoods. And of course talk of God invariably includes talk about everything else—life, faith, doubt, being a neighbor, parent, sister, brother, spouse, citizen, about what it means to be human.

In the past we've typically assumed that if you want to find God, go- ing to church is the place to go. I wonder if this is still the case. It seems to me that God is breaking out of churches everywhere. In fact, some would say that's not the best place to find him. Given the places Jesus frequented, that shouldn't surprise us (hint: he never went to church!). It turns out that a pub creates a perfect setting in which to encounter people who are interested in spiritual topics, philosophy, life, and—yes—theology, and they are open to being honest about it. For some, it even becomes a place to encounter God himself.

Let me be up front that I write this as a Christian. But I write in the hope that readers of any perspective, religious or not, might garner something from these pages. Further, my hope is that as you read you will encounter a shift toward a more chastened, humble, and inviting

Christianity—one that will have a seat at the table in the important conversations our world is having. Unless we are willing to first listen and make space for the other, we won't be invited. Here you will find real life stories, real people, real questions—many gleaned from conversations and encounters during actual Pub Theology gatherings. These recollections will attempt to give flesh and bones to this needed shift.

Where is God?

Who is God?

What do other religions say?

What do those who've given up on God say?

Turns out agnostics, atheists, Buddhists, Hindus, humanists, Jews, Muslims, Wiccans, and many others have wonderful traditions that have wrestled with these very questions for centuries. It's time we start to listen. If you're tired of pat answers that exclude wrestling and doubt while presuming certainty in the face of serious questions, welcome to the club. I wrestle with these issues in my own life. I wouldn't be surprised if you do as well. I hope you'll find encouragement and ideas here toward living out a more global faith.

Whether we all agree with each other is not the issue. The reality is the plurality that is there. We cannot escape this, as Wilfred Cantwell Smith noted so aptly back in the sixties:

> The religious life of mankind from now on, if it is to be lived at all, will be lived in a context of religious pluralism. . . . This is true for all of us; not only for "mankind" in general on an abstract level, but for you and me as individual persons. No longer are people of other persuasions peripheral or distant, the idle curiosities of travelers' tales. The more alert we are, and the more involved in life, the more we are finding that they are our neighbors, our colleagues, our competitors, our fellows. Confucians and Hindus, Buddhists and Muslims, are with us not only in the United Nations, but down the street. Increasingly, not only is our civilization's destiny affected by their actions; but we drink coffee with them as well.[1]

The reality is, other religious approaches increasingly surround us, not to mention the rise of people claiming no religious affiliation at all. One's faith cannot exist in a vacuum—not if it hopes to be a part of the global conversation. This presents an opportunity for engagement, a necessary engagement. As Paul Knitter noted so appropriately over a dozen

---

1. Quoted in Knitter, *Theologies of Religions*, 5.

years ago: "Two of the greatest threats facing the community of nations and cultures are the nationalism and fanaticism that grow among those who have never left their village and who think that it is superior to all others."[2] It is amazing to think that this could still be the case in our world today given the technologies that are constantly shrinking our world. But the truth is, you can be connected through the world via the Internet, and visit the same old sites that reinforce your worldview. You could live next door to a Buddhist family from Laos, but if you only go past their house to get to your church, and never take a side trip to the neighboring porch, you'll simply reinforce your own ways of thinking. It's time to leave the village, which—believe it or not—may be as simple as going next door.

I'll be honest—the above episode with a local pastor surprised me. Surely pastors are open people. Surely good, Christian people are open. Well, perhaps we aren't as open as we like to think, after all. And that includes me. This episode served as a reminder of how far we Christians have to go in learning to truly see one another as fellow human beings created in God's image. When we struggle to even live up to our own theology, we may find ourselves in a very precarious position in diminishing the theology of others. It's time we move from fear to openness. From building walls to seeking hospitality. Fidelity to Jesus—who constantly made space for those who didn't fit religiously, culturally, morally, and otherwise—demands nothing less.

And so precisely because I am a Christian, because I follow Jesus, I must be one who shares the religious space in my community with others, indeed, even become a learner at their feet. This book explains one person's experience in seeking to do just that.

2. Ibid., 12.

1

Before the Pub

You may rejoice to think yourselves secure,
You may be grateful for the gift divine—
That grace unsought, which made your black hearts pure,
And fits your earth-born souls in Heaven to shine.
But is it sweet to look around and view
Thousands excluded from that happiness,
Which they deserve at least as much as you,
Their faults not greater nor their virtues less?

— Anne Brontë, "A Word to the Elect"

There's nothing I love more than honest conversation with people about things that matter. This includes those who think differently than I do. It is endlessly fascinating to learn how people see the world, how it shapes their lives, their choices, their hopes, their relationships— what they *do*. I have a lot to learn from others. As a pastor, in some ways I get paid to talk. To tell people what I think. But my first enjoyment is learning from others—especially people with vastly different experiences and perspectives on life. It enriches me. But at this point you may be wondering: who is this pastor who likes to drink beer and thinks we ought to listen to what atheists and Muslims have to say? He must have grown up in a pretty liberal and godless environment. Not even close.

I grew up in the church. I attended Sunday school, vacation Bible school, the works, all from a very young age. I knew that God existed, that Jesus loved me, and that doing bad things was a bad idea. It all seemed pretty straightforward and—in many ways—was simply taken for granted. These things are obvious things—and everyone believes them. We were like a school of fish swimming in Jesus water. We were oblivious to what we were swimming in, and assumed that the way we perceived our world was simply the way the world *is*.

In the back of my mind I was aware that there were people who didn't go to church, or who perhaps belonged to different religions, but they were outside my realm of reality, hence, outside of reality altogether for me. In our own small town I knew there were people who didn't go to church, but I had no idea what they thought or why. I just knew that we generally considered them "not good people." The good people go to church. Of course. How this squared with the fact that we were supposed to be sharing the love of Jesus with these same people wasn't my business to figure out. They were bad, we were good, and oh right, I suppose we should invite them to that church potluck on Friday evening. What these people actually thought was way beyond me, and frankly I never considered it. But the truth is, that up until high school, I'm not sure how much I thought about what I believed either.

So it was something of a shock when I learned for the first time what it was that we actually believed. In our tradition, the Reformed faith, we believed things as a community—which in many ways is a healthy and helpful antidote to the surfeit of individualism in our culture. We were a community that belonged to a larger community. One with a history and deep roots. One that could take pride in its theological heritage and its faithfulness to God over the years. This is a very good thing. Its downside, however, is that it discourages individuals from questioning what the community has always believed—and in many ways has taken for granted. Little fishes aren't supposed to notice the water.

Like many, I was born into the church. In other words, I was born into a church-going family, and in our tradition, we baptize babies—often in the first several months of life. This is a sort of communal initiation into the community, somewhat analogous to circumcision in Judaism. The beauty of this practice is that it cuts through some of the individualism that is pervasive in a culture of "me and Jesus" and "my personal decision" and "my spirituality." We were part of a community. We surrendered our autonomy at some level to the community of faith around us. A beautiful thing in many, many ways.

In this context, it is assumed that at some point you will articulate your own faith. You will display that your initiation into the faith community as an infant was not a fluke, was not somehow misguided, but was in fact the initial step in a process that is continuing until now. At this point, when you are of sufficient maturity, you will stand in front of the whole church and make profession of faith—preferably before you are done with high school, if all goes "according to plan." (See my wife's upcoming book, *Cracking the Pot,* for an inside account of this process.)

What is a profession of faith? At a base level it involves answering a few questions about God correctly. At an ideal level it is taking ownership of what you believe in. For us, that couldn't happen without regurgitating a certain amount of abstruse theological concepts. And truth be told, it seems many made a profession of faith for the sake of making everyone in the congregation relax, not least the parents!

"Phew, the next generation is still with us."

"Good, the little fishy has learned to swim."

If you wanted to stay on everyone's good side, it was the thing to do. So it became my turn. I was in my senior year of high school and everyone would "feel a lot better" if I made profession of faith before heading off to college. No problem. I certainly felt confident to articulate what I believed about God. I had been taught well. The pastor came over to our house to go over the basics of our doctrine, so that I could answer the questions correctly in front of the church elders. At some point the topic of predestination came up.

"Bryan, listen. Grace is so great, because God *chose* us before the world began."

"So I had nothing to do with it?"

"Yes! Exactly—it is all a gift from God."

"That's wonderful. God is good! But wait, what about other people?"

"What other people?"

"The people God didn't choose."

"Well, he did choose them."

"What do you mean?"

"He chose them to spend eternity apart from him."

I shifted uncomfortably in my chair. "Wait a second. I think I get God choosing people as his own. But he really chooses other people to go to hell?"

He smiled. Pastors love a good theological conversation. I should know. "Bryan, it's all about God. Not us. That's the beauty of the Reformed faith. God gets the glory. God chose some to receive his grace, and by necessity, that means he also chose some not to."

I took a swig of water from my glass. Was it getting warmer in here? I had to get this straight: "So God decided before anyone was born whether they would go to heaven or to hell?"

He didn't hesitate: "Yes."

I was nearly sick about this. God decided to send people to hell before they were born? How is that fair? How does that even make sense? How is that a God of love? How is that not worse than the worst thing anyone can imagine? It was a bitter pill to swallow, but who was I to question centuries-old dogma? And besides, I did really want to know the truth, even if it was ugly.

"All right."

But that ugly feeling never went away. It took years before I was able to properly begin to dissect this kind of theology. Because in our tradition, you don't question the theology. You just learn it. You certainly don't question God. Because he's *GAWD*. (Said with a deep, profound, preacher-voice.)

The tradition I grew up in—the Christian Reformed Church—prides itself on its ethnic identity, being historically comprised of largely Dutch immigrants, with its historical and theological roots coming from John Calvin and the Reformation. We even have a college and seminary named after him. Perhaps you've heard of them. We take pride in knowing our theology, and knowing it well. It's a beautiful tradition—a wonderful tradition—for which I am very grateful. It is one that has shaped and continues to shape me in important ways.

One of the things about having such a robust theological tradition, however, is that we don't think we have much to learn from anyone else. We have the truth, after all. I mean, Calvin wrote the *Institutes*—what else is there? Now it's just a matter of memorizing it as best you can (not to mention trying to apply archaic late-medieval metaphysics to your life today). Simple, right?

There was a pervading sense of something like the following: we think we pretty much know everything there is to know, at least of whatever is actually worth knowing. I'm not sure I could have identified this sense growing up (it's always hard to see the water you're swimming in), but certainly looking back it is clear that this line of thinking was (and still is) quite pervasive. We have the right view of just about everything: politics, the environment, family, the economy, how to plant a garden, social etiquette, how often to wash the bed sheets, etc. We've got an outlook on life, and not only does it work for us, but we think it would work for pretty much everyone else as well. Why? Because it's the right view.

So growing up, curiosity was not exactly encouraged. Especially theological curiosity. Whenever one of us in Sunday school would ask, "Where did Cain get his wife?" or "Why did Jesus say only God is good? I thought Jesus *was* God." The response would be a variation of the following (explicitly or implicitly): "Just learn what we teach you, and never mind asking why." And if you asked why? "Because we said so." Really not a bad system as long as everyone does what he or she is told.

I don't want you to think I regret or even despise my theological roots. Far from it. It is a very deep, rich tradition. Some of the foibles I mention here could just as well apply to many other traditions. Perhaps even yours.

I wonder if part of the reason we all continued to think the same is that we had never been introduced to people who thought differently. Anne Bronte's "A Word to the Elect" (originally titled "A Word to the Calvinists") was not on our recommended reading list. Perhaps for good reason. Because then we'd have to think seriously about what we believed, and thinking seriously about what you believe always entails the risk that you might realize what you have believed may not be in harmony with how things actually are. But it seems we have more invested in maintaining our view of things than actually seeking the truth, despite numerous professions of ardently doing the latter.

If people who thought differently were mentioned at all, it was in light of their errors. For example, Jacobus Arminius—a sixteenth-century heretic in the Netherlands— was mentioned only because he was so wrong (and we wouldn't have the Canons of Dort without him). Never mind honestly pursuing what he actually said and matching that up with the text and the tradition. Don't get me wrong—in Arminius' day there certainly was much deep thinking and wrestling with his arguments, but over time we forget why something is wrong and it has ossified into something that is simply axiomatic. It is apparently convenient to have a few examples of those who tried to take another path but were duly "corrected." They become scapegoats and examples of what happens to those who question the status quo, and scare the rest of the flock into more mindless munching of grass that no longer grows.

We knew how to argue theologically against Arminians (God chooses us, not vice versa), Baptists (splash 'em when they're young), Catholics (they had failed to read the 95 theses), Lutherans (they made a religion out of the 95 theses), Episcopalians (too liturgical), Evangelicals (not liturgical enough), Methodists (they were too socially concerned), Charismatics (too excited), and any other sort of Christian who dared to challenge our theological supremacy. We even felt we were better— and more right!— than our sister denomination, the Reformed Church in America, which also began with a group of Dutch immigrants. Other religions were, of course, not even worthy of mention. We were right, and we had the documentation to prove it. Out of all the billions of human beings who had ever lived, of varying languages, ethnicities, religions, God had seen fit to give us (*us!*)—a small group of people mostly concentrated in West Michigan—the corner on him. Amazing. And as for arrogance, well, it isn't arrogance if you're right.

Yet at some point along the path, I began to feel that theology is not simply archival. It is *not* just a matter of looking up how the answers were pounded out at the sixth council in Constantinople or in the sixteen hundreds in Europe. If humanity is learning and growing all the time in its understanding of the world and of itself, might it be possible that we have more to learn about God? I had a growing hunch that the answer was yes. This little fishy had finally noticed the water. And what I started noticing, as I began to trust my own fins, was the fact that we weren't living in a fishbowl, but in an awfully big pond. In fact, you might even call it an ocean.

2

Setting the Table

I've heard to have happiness, you must believe
if we all have the same ideals, we'll live in harmony
well sure this sounds nice, but take a closer look
if you're not a mystic, you're living your life by a book

peacefulness and happiness is our common goal
but there is much darkness before the end of the tunnel

I'm told materialism is just man's evil
I often feel the same about the supernatural
I can't deal with the closed minds of those who know it all
everyone wants their answer to be the one for us to follow

I'm standing on my rock, no better than anyone else
giving my piece to the puzzle that will never be solved
until we can respect what one another think
we'll be trapped on this boat just now starting to sink

—Derek del Barrio

BABY STEPS

So you're still waiting for me to get to the beer. Don't let me stop you. Grab a brew, and strap in for another chapter. We're getting there! First, we have to connect a few more dots. How did I break out of the fishbowl of my youth? What was it like to come across strange fish, bigger fish from bigger ponds, even atheist fish? In other words, how in the world did I go from my comfortable, familiar theological fishbowl to a bigger pond, a place that even made something like Pub Theology possible?

Armed with a secure view of the world—much of which I still hold dear—I was sent off to college at the University of Michigan. (Where, perhaps ironically, there was an academic building nicknamed "the Fishbowl.") There I began running into people I had only marginally heard of growing up: Hindus, Muslims, Jews, homosexuals, agnostics, and, gasp . . . atheists! But I wasn't totally ready for it. So I found refuge in a primarily Caucasian evangelical campus ministry, which, while being more diverse theologically than my upbringing, was familiar enough to be comforting. The main difference in this group was the hyper-evangelical obsession with trying to convert everyone to "our way of seeing" things by actually going out and knocking on doors. (Contrasted with being content to sit on the couch and rejoice in "our way of seeing" things.) Perhaps you have been involved in such a group yourself, or been the surprising recipient of such a knock on the door. Calvinists don't bother with all that, because God has made all the decisions already anyway.

Now I was actually meeting people with vastly different views, yet I wasn't ready to approach these relationships as a learner. At the same time, a small but important opening had begun—I was finally interacting with people who thought differently than I did. (Don't laugh—this is a step that many have simply never taken.) This fishy began to realize that the world wasn't made up solely of goldfish (or blonde-haired, blue-eyed fish).

After awhile I even began to befriend these formerly off-limits people. I had a roommate who was Catholic (baby steps). A classmate who was a Hindu became a friend (we spent countless hours playing cards in the dorms). I became a Resident Assistant (RA) in a dorm on campus and had fellow RAs who were Jewish, gay, and atheists. And—surprise!—it turned out they weren't totally different. In fact, they weren't that different at all. We shared something inescapable: our humanity.

LEARNING TO LEARN

Fast forward. At some point along the way, I decided to become a preacher. Crazy, yes. But I assume God had to be involved at some level, because this was a miracle of no small proportions. I was the kid who, as a freshman in high school, was so shy that if you even looked at me, my eyes would start welling up with tears and I would embarrassingly swim the other way before you tried to talk to me. Somehow I enrolled in seminary anyway. Call it a death-wish if you like.

Well, after spending the prerequisite amount of time at the aptly named Calvin Seminary, I was sent out to gather other goldfish and remind them of how great our bowl was. At seminary I was reintroduced to some of the doctrines I grew up with, which after spending some time in fundamentalist evangelical circles for years was actually a welcome respite and gladly familiar. I also, however, learned that there were parts of my Reformed theological tradition that were much broader than what I grew up with (or somehow I missed them the first time around!). Insights from Abraham Kuyper on the belief that Jesus Christ was Lord not just of my little group, but of the whole earth called for a serious cultural engagement, not a retreat into a firmly entrenched corner. This brought with it an openness, an excitement that I desperately needed. I was reminded that the secular-sacred dualism we often assume in popular Christianity is a bit of a false dichotomy. Evangelicals I had been around for the past number of years were scared of "the world" and this fit well with what I had been around growing up. However, a healthy, robust Reformed approach to life wasn't scared of anything—because it was all God's! It ought to be approached by faith, and by an understanding that God cares not just about human souls but about the entire physical creation he has made. This was a theology I could get behind, and as I studied, seemed to be rooted firmly in the text.

As graduation neared, my wife and I began to wonder where we might end up as far as a job. There was no shortage of churches that were vacant (apparently becoming a pastor is not quite the highly-sought-after occupation it used to be). After giving it a lot of thought and prayer, we felt that walking into an established church would force us to "do it the way it's always been done." This lack of creativity was basically what we'd been doing our whole lives already. Maybe it was time for a change. We decided, with prayer and an unexpected leading of the Holy Spirit, to start something new.

Out of this was born a small community of faith. A group of people began to gather. People who, for the most part, weren't indoctrinated into one Christian worldview or another. Or if they were, they were seeking change as well. Here were people who didn't walk in the door having all the answers and no questions, but who brought their own life experiences, brokenness and, yes, even questions. It was great. We were tempted just to extend the party line and get them up to speed on obscure theological arguments from the Middle Ages, but decided against it (another gift of the Holy Spirit). Rather, we decided to listen. To learn. And to realize that part of being a genuine community of any sort (church or otherwise) required that we approach one another prepared to learn. That was a new concept for us, but it was great. And we began to learn that there were other ways to think about God, other ways to worship, other historic Christian traditions (that we'd smugly dismissed before) that had incredible depth and value.

Now we incorporated Catholic hymns, Methodist prayers, practices and sayings from the Desert Fathers, experiential spirituality from Eastern traditions. In other words, we were beginning to delve into a well that was much deeper than we had realized. This was something that began to feed us in a profound way. We were hungry for depth, and it turns out, diversity is something that adds texture, life, and even spice to what can become the routine and familiar. We were stumbling into what Brian McLaren so aptly calls "a generous orthodoxy." New traditions were not something to be afraid of, or defend the truth against, or speak ill of. They were, rather, our brothers and sisters in Christ throughout history and throughout the world who brought something to the table that we desperately needed. We were beginning to sense what Paul meant when he said, "in fact, God has arranged the parts in the body, every one of them, just as he wanted them to be" and that "if one part is honored, every part rejoices with it" (1 Cor 12:18, 26).

Eventually this small but growing community began to wonder how we could extend this desire to learn beyond our own doors. We figured there were other people out there who had an interest in God and spirituality, but had no interest in church for whatever reason (who could imagine?). I had heard of a church in London doing pub gatherings, and I liked how they phrased it: "Some of the most important moments in the history of the church took place in the pub. Luther kick started the Reformation over a few pints. The Church of England was started in the white horse tavern. Hymns like 'Love Divine, All Loves Excelling' were inspired by pub music. And seemingly all the best conversations take place in the pub. The format is simple: beer, conversation, and God. Everything is up for discussion, no assumptions, no barriers to entry. If you are going to get upset because someone questions something that is important to you maybe this isn't for you, but if you think that whatever might be true ought to be able to stand up to being questioned, maybe it is."[1]

Here was a chance to engage with the broader diversity around us— not only Christians from other traditions, but Hindus, Buddhists, Jews, Muslims, atheists, humanists, whoever! Some would look at this primarily as an "outreach" ministry. And it certainly can be that, and perhaps for our friends in London it was intended to be just that. However, I took it another way. Here was a chance for me to learn, to grow, and expand. I guess I'm just selfish that way. I love to learn (and I kinda love beer), so it seemed a good idea. So it is helpful as we continue that I clarify that—at least in our instance—this is not the latest and greatest evangelism fad, or a way to get people on the street into our church. Those things may happen, but the intent is simply to grow, to learn, and to perhaps make some new friends along the way.

And the more I considered it, the more it seemed obvious: how could you go wrong with beer, conversation and God? Two out of those three usually work pretty well, I figured, so perhaps all three might be a perfect little trifecta.

I was not wrong.

---

1. churchonthecorner.org.uk

3

Opening Night

I would like to have the men of Heaven in my own house:
With vats of good cheer laid out for them.
I would like to have the three Marys, their fame is so great.
I would like people from every corner of Heaven.
I would like them to be cheerful in their drinking,
I would like to have Jesus, too, here amongst them.
I would like a great lake of beer for the King of Kings,
I would like to be watching Heaven's family, drinking it through all eternity.

—St. Brigid

THE GO AHEAD

Pub Theology. Talking about God over a beer. It sounded too good to be true. What would other churches think? What would the higher-ups in my denomination think? Would I be reprimanded? Was this really appropriate? A pastor hanging out drinking beer at the local bar under the pretext of discussing theology? There would be skeptics. But I knew we had stumbled onto something. After all, the church has quite a history with beer and brewing. Many of the early Christians—standing in the Hellenistic/Judaic tradition—scorned beer and brewing. Yet in Ireland, which was never under Roman rule, another practice developed.

There, beer played a significant role, notes Franz Meussdoerffer in his *Comprehensive History of Beer Brewing.*[1]

Irish missionaries like St. Columbanus spread the Celtic predilection for beer as well as the Christian faith throughout Europe. Columbanus was even said to perform "beer miracles." So the attitude of the church toward beer began to change in the sixth and seventh centuries as the Germanic and Celtic traditions began to spread. (We should acknowledge, however, that some churches are still about fifteen centuries behind this development!) Meussdoerffer notes that the documented recognition of beer by the church, however, only came in the year 816 at the Synod of Aachen, where a standardized binding order of monastery life was deliberated. It was decided that a monk should receive daily one beaker of wine or, where no wine was available, twice as much of "good beer."[2]

In time, monasteries became brewing centers, and it was in a monastery where hops were first introduced into the mix. In short, beer and the church go way back. "We really could do this," I thought to myself. "And I know just the place." There was a new place in town that brewed their own beer, and had a reputation not only for tasty brews using largely local hops and other local ingredients, but for being an eclectic, unusual place. It was in the warehouse district of town (a very small section of our non-industrial northern Michigan town). Were there even warehouses there? Maybe one. No, there had to be at least two if it had earned the name "district." Anyway, I hadn't been to this place before, but had heard from friends that it was worth checking out. I actually had been to the building it was in, but that was years before the brewery was put in. When the warehouse had been cleared out and cleaned up, we had checked it out as a possible place to gather our faith community. The rent was a bit high and we landed elsewhere (in a former mental hospital—a clear upgrade!—and a whole other story).

Approaching this former warehouse now, it was clearly a different place. Walls had been put in. Cement floors with an orange-brown glazing. They had created an industrial feel with exposed ceiling, pipes, and ductwork. A nice mix of wood, metal, and art. Fairly bright for such a place, and open, with regular tables and chairs arranged in the middle of the room, and an occasional couch or former hospital chair. Turning my

1. Meussdoerffer, "A Comprehensive History of Beer Brewing," 10.
2. Ibid.

gaze toward the beer menu, I thought I saw something out of the corner of my eye. I did a double-take. Yup, an old church pew along the far wall. Sweet. A sign, perhaps?

I walked up to the counter. "Is Russ here?" I had been told who to ask for.

"Russ? He's around here somewhere."

"Can I talk to him?"

"Hold on a minute."

I looked around at the place. It was mid-afternoon. The front end of happy hour. A few folks were hanging about the place. Some wearing business wear—a few suits and ties—others, jeans and casual, a few looked like they had biked in, wearing cycling gear. It was a comfortable place. A few random pieces of art on the wall and hanging from the ceiling—hues of green and orange on the walls, including a wall made up entirely of hand-painted members' mugs, which each member of the brewery was able to decorate as they liked. It was eclectic, unique, good. A couple of old hospital chairs offset the typical black steel and wood tables setup throughout—and of course, an old church pew. No TV sets to distract the eye, good music over the sound system, conversation in the air—I liked it.

"What can I do for you?"

I turned and saw a shorter man, about my age—mid thirties—wearing black designer glasses and a t-shirt.

"Are you Russ?"

"Yeah. That's me."

"Hey, I'm Bryan."

"What can I do for you?"

"Well, I had this idea about a gathering. It's a conversation group, and it's about three things: beer, conversation, and God." I showed him a mock-up poster I had made. "There's a church in London doing something like this, and we thought it'd be cool to have something like this going in Traverse City."

"Tell me more about it."

"Well, the idea is to get people of different perspectives and beliefs around the table, and, in a great setting like this, have discussion about stuff like religion, faith, life, and so on. It's not a Bible study, it's not even really a church gathering, per se. Just a group of people who are interested in what other people think on these issues."

"And you thought you could meet here."

"Yeah, we think your place fits the bill. We were thinking Thursday nights. Eight or eight thirty until whenever we finish."

"OK."

"OK? We can do it?"

"Yeah—give it a shot. Sounds interesting."

"Great. Do you mind if I put up a few posters like this one to let people know about it?"

"Go ahead—let me know if you need anything."

So we were in. Just like that. Right Brain Brewery—the name alone was promising. Now Russ is no fool, his business has expanded quite a bit since they initially opened, including a recent mention in the *New York Times*. You can now find a draft or two of theirs on tap at many area restaurants and bars. From his perspective, a weekly discussion group meant consistent business, possibly new business. But his openness to a group of our sort was certainly appreciated. He could have been wary of a group discussing potentially volatile subjects over alcohol—but if he had such reservations, he kept them to himself.

SOMETHING NEW IS BORN

We set the date. October 16. That gave us a couple of weeks to get the word out, to put some posters up. It was time to get this thing rolling. When I told folks in our community about this—to this point I had pursued the idea on my own—they were pumped.

A few reactions:

"Uhmmm . . . let me think . . . beer, conversation and God. What's not to like?! I believe that we will be there! Although . . . right brain and theology . . . either it's a good balance or the universe is going to implode."

"Count me in next week! I am heading to Dallas today. I love the sound of this!"

"My wife just called me to tell me how 'cool' this is! She can't wait to go. I will forward this to my daughter too."

"Wow. This is great you guys! I wish I could reply (online) to every one of the discussion topics, but it'd take all day! Just wanted to encourage all of you who are getting (and keeping) conversations going out there!"

With much anticipation we printed up some posters, put them around town, and began to spread the word. Much of the early buzz reflected the quotes you just read. But does excitement translate to people actually showing up? It was about a month between the initial idea and our first gathering. As we neared the event and continued to receive such positive feedback, my excitement grew more and more. I knew it was going to be a great thing—I just couldn't wait for the first night. Who would show up? How would conversation go? How many people would there be? Would we fit at one table? Would people be willing to talk? To be honest?

I was ready. But life was continuing outside of this new reality we were soon to experience—turns out another new reality was on the plate for my family. My wife was pregnant at the time, and her due date was October 13, or three days before our first gathering, scheduled for the 16th. I had jokingly asked her to either hurry up and have the baby on time, or wait until Thursday was over. Our baby had other plans.

So at 7:15 in the morning, the day of the event, Josephine Rae was born. My little girl. We had three boys at this point, so this was quite a new thing for us—a little one in pink. It was incredible. The brothers all came up and fawned over their new little sister. I stayed by mom's side, never of course bringing up the fact that there was this event going on that night. That was the last thing on my wife's mind. We were celebrating. Our baby girl was here. And aside from that, she was recovering from giving birth. No small thing. (As if I have any clue.)

Our gathering was to start at 8:30pm. It was early afternoon. Well-wishers came by, we changed the baby's first diaper. We downloaded a bunch of songs with "Josephine" in them (there are quite a few!), and we rested all afternoon enjoying the sights and sounds of our baby girl.

Evening arrived. We ordered hospital room service for dinner. I wondered about the rest of the evening. My event was finally here. I was supposed to facilitate. Was I going to have to miss it? I could hardly bear the thought. I had been waiting for this night for weeks! But I couldn't just leave my wife and newborn, could I? After our dinner came, and our girl was resting comfortably in momma's arms . . . I decided to open my mouth.

"So, you've got things under control pretty well here."

"Yeah—I guess this gets easier the fourth time around," she laughed.

I was quick to respond: "Too bad, cuz there's not gonna be another!"

"You got that right!"

Josephine made a small gurgling sound—no doubt triumphing in her status as only daughter and youngest—a potentially troublesome combination!

"So, do you need anything?"

"No."

"You comfortable?"

"Yes." Josephine murmured in momma's arms. "Isn't she sweet?"

"The sweetest."

"I can't get over it—a little girl!"

OK, here goes, I thought. "So . . . I was thinking . . . our first gathering at the pub is tonight."

"Oh that's right."

Time to drop the bomb, "You wouldn't mind if I stopped in for a bit, would you?"

Pause.

"No, of course not—we're all set. Grandma has the boys. I've got the nurses here to help if I need anything. You should be there."

Are you kidding?! My wife is the best. "You're the best."

"I know," she smiled.

And so I left my newborn baby daughter and my post-partum wife and headed out for a beer. What kind of a husband does this? I got to the pub a few minutes early. I beat the crowd. If, in fact, a crowd was even coming. I was excited—I just had a baby girl! I was excited—our first night of Pub Theology had finally arrived! I floated into the pub, with visions of newness dancing in my head.

I stepped up to the bar.

"I just had a baby." Who could keep from sharing news like this?

"Really?"

"Well, my wife did." Clarification.

"Congratulations."

"A little girl—our first girl after three boys."

"Well, this one's on the house. What'll you have?"

4

A Story of Two Tables

Say, does your heart expand to all mankind?
And, would you ever to your neighbour do—
The weak, the strong, the enlightened, and the blind—
As you would have your neighbour do to you?

And, when you, looking on your fellow-men,
Behold them doomed to endless misery,
How can you talk of joy and rapture then?—
May God withhold such cruel joy from me!

—Anne Brontë, 'A Word to the Elect'

TABLE ONE

Arriving at the pub on a discussion night always brings with it a sense of anticipation. Who will show up tonight? Will it go well? Will people talk? Will they like it? I usually arrive, target a couple of open tables (now we actually have our own reserved large table), set down the sheets of questions for the night, and grab a pint. On a particular night some months into our project, I returned to my seat with a delicious brew called "Ethel the Frog ESB" (that's Extra Special Bitter for you non-beer drinkers). I saw some new faces and realized the tables were filling up quickly. It was going to be a good night.

When the crowd reaches a certain size, over a dozen or so, it is not unusual for us to split into a couple of groups, so that everyone can participate in the conversation. This was one of those evenings. So we split up the tables, and people found their way into one group or another. The people at my table were engaging in some light conversation and introducing themselves to each other. In the middle of this I noticed someone join the other group. A heavier-set fellow, hair a bit disheveled and peering out of thick glasses, lumbered over to the other group. Interestingly, I noticed he had his hands full. But instead of holding a beer, he was holding several large books, and some papers on top of that. I didn't give it much more thought, and turned my attention to our own group.

We had great conversation on such topics as: "Do you prefer to think about faith as mainly about facts or about mystery?" and "Is it more important to believe the right things or to do the right things?" and "How do you know that you actually exist?" You laugh—but this last question can generate very interesting discussion, particularly after a couple of pints. Most people at the table indicated that faith seems somewhat mysterious to them, and that limiting it to facts seems to take the hope or life out of it. A person with Buddhist leanings noted that it is all ultimately mystery, and that facts are a matter of perception when it comes to issues of faith. A Christian at the table challenged that view, noting that Christianity is a historical religion, unlike Buddhism, and has its roots in actual historical events, i.e. facts. I sat back, enjoying my extra special bitter ale and listening to the discussion going on around me. I thought, this is what it's all about: people of diverse backgrounds, experiences, and religious perspectives all sitting at the same table, having a rich, meaningful, and respectful conversation, even as differences of opinions are voiced. It *is* a good night.

THAT FIRST NIGHT

So what happened that first night—when I fled the delivery room in order to drink beer and talk about God? Did anyone come? Was it a complete flop? Did my wife speak to me again? Will my daughter ever recover from those precious early hours not spent with her dad? Will she need counseling in the future? These are great questions—hey, we should meet at the pub to discuss them!

In all seriousness, what did happen? Well, for one thing, it's hard to remember that far back. My recollection of that first evening goes like this:

a nice number of people turned out—maybe a dozen, maybe 15. It turned out it was all people I already knew, and all of them were Christians of one sort or another. In fact, many of them went to my church. So the evening entailed a lot of chit-chat and people catching up on their week. OK. So how do we transition to talking about theology? How do you interrupt someone sharing about how her boss gave her an impossible assignment to say, "I'm sorry, do you think God is omnipotent, and if so, why didn't he stop your boss from doing that?" Followed by, "If so, why does God allow earthquakes and tsunamis to happen, in which countless innocents die?" It just isn't easy to do.

Our regular practice now is to have some topics chosen ahead of time to discuss. That first night I hadn't thought to bring any. Cut me some slack, I had a daughter that day! Actually my wife did all the work, but you know what I mean. I think somehow I believed that we would all show up and immediately dive into the depths of divine mysteries. So I said, "Who's got a question or a deep topic for us to discuss?" Crickets. Nothing. Hmmm . . . This was going to be harder than I thought. I had assumed we'd all show up and instantly be engaging the difference between Luther and Zwingli's understanding of the Lord's Supper and whether or not it mattered. We ended up talking about a few things here and there, the exact topics remain somewhat elusive to me, but I recall thinking—there has to at least be some direction here. And we need some nonbelievers or adherents of other religions.

So going forward, we worked to connect with new people, so it wouldn't be basically a church small group meeting at the pub. A church small group was *not* what I had envisioned. By putting up a few more posters and having people inviting coworkers and friends from their neighborhoods, we were able to get a few people of differing perspectives at future gatherings. That helped. A lot. Also, from that point forward, I began to bring a list of questions or topics. This has come to be known as "the sheet." The sheet usually has five to eight topics on spiritual, religious, political, or other life concerns. It might be a question. It might be a provocative quote. It might be a poem. I try to allow a variety of perspectives to be represented on the sheet, so that even if we don't have an atheist or Muslim at the table, we are forced to interact with some of their views, and they have at last some voice in the discussion.

What I tell people each week is that the topics on the sheet are not an end in themselves. They are merely a jumping off point, conversation starters, if you will. If they are interesting and we stay on a particular topic, great. If that topic leads us somewhere else that has people's interest, great. I don't come needing the discussion to go here or there, and try not to come covertly plotting to steer the conversation in any one direction. That would be underhanded and could possibly shortcut true, open dialogue. I am there to learn, question and wonder, and if asked, give my opinion. Not everyone comes with this mindset however. Why not? Why are we often so quick to speak and slow to listen?

TARGET PRACTICE

On the positive side of this question—why we are so quick to speak—we may note that there is genuine earnestness to share what one loves. Just as one is quick to share a love of food, or sports, or gardening, so one who deeply values her faith will be eager to share it with others. This is not a bad thing. In fact, it's a very good thing, and it's part of being human.

On the other side of the question, it seems that something has happened to the gospel itself. Or better, something has altered what many people perceive the gospel to be. In many evangelical settings, it might be said that the gospel has become an end in itself. In other words, the point of believing the gospel gets reduced to turning one into a person who tells other people about it. The content is almost forgotten in one's zeal to "get the word out." Getting the word out becomes the point.

In college I hung out with a group that took this very seriously. You were to share the gospel with your roommates, your classmates, the guy working at the campus book store, the girl who is selling your coffee, the lady serving lunch in the dorm. Everyone is a potential target. And target is a good word.

My first connection with this group started this way: "If you want to be in a Bible study with us, you have to commit to sharing the gospel with everyone who lives on your hall before the end of the first semester." Sounded great, except that I was hoping to become friends with some of them. Many of these folks were so "on fire" for sharing the good news that if you looked them in the eye while walking to class, they'd take that as a sign that you were ready to pray the "sinner's prayer." After knocking on about 100 doors and handing out thousands of "spiritual interest" surveys, I began to get pretty good at it. Some people even prayed the prayer with me. In retrospect, I realized that this constant need to evangelize, and the obsession with learning methodology and answers to questions was little more than a sales routine. It was a scheme to get more people involved in our little campus group, and the bigger that got, the more important we felt on campus. And of course it was ultimately about serving God, which makes the whole thing not just OK, but necessary.

I have mostly recovered from this habit of seeing people as targets to shoot with my gospel artillery. Naïvely, I sort of assumed everyone else had too. The approach began to "seem so yesterday" as I thought about it. But then, yesterday, I went to a gathering of church planters and pastors who are starting new churches. The focus of the meeting was on evangelism. Great, I thought, I wonder what new approaches they will discuss. I anticipated hearing something new and nuanced about appreciating the other person's perspective, about learning from them and investing in a relationship, and about allowing natural conversations to happen when it comes up, rather than forcing our agenda inappropriately.

I was quite disappointed.

No new methods. No nuance. Just an encouragement to learn one particular "method" such as is outlined in various literature and tracts, memorize it, and then "train, train, train." It sounded an awful lot like what the management at the local Kia dealership does in training its sales force.

Unsurprisingly, some people with this understanding of the gospel show up at Pub Theology. Which brings us back to that other table.

TABLE TWO

That night—after we'd been going a few months—I glanced over at the other table, and noticed that the larger fellow with a stack of books was talking somewhat heatedly, and had begun handing out some pieces of paper. I returned my attention to our group. The question before us asked: "Is it more important to do the right things, or believe the right things?"

Nearly everyone at our table—an atheist, an agnostic, a spiritual-but-not-religious-type with Buddhist leanings, and several folks of varying Christian affiliation— felt that at the end of the day, it is more important to do the right things than to believe the right things. On the one hand, I was not surprised at all. Most people agree that talk is cheap, and that at the end of the day, how you live your life, what you do, is what matters most. But this is a very materialist view of things. It's grounded in the physical, the material, the concrete. I thought perhaps I would hear a few of the Christians voice the traditional "if you don't believe the right things you won't go to heaven" line. When it didn't come out, I decided to voice it. It was countered, by a Christian of all people, with a line from Jesus in Matthew 25: "I tell you the truth, whatever you did not do for one of the least of these, you did not do for me." Then they will go away to eternal punishment, but the righteous (those who *did* the right things), will go to eternal life." Murmurs of "Wow," "That's right," and "Damn straight!" were heard around the table. Quoting Jesus always goes a long way, even with atheists.

I noticed someone get up and leave the other table, someone whom I hadn't seen at any previous Pub Theology gatherings. As far as I could tell, our friend with the books was still holding court and talking. I had a notion that our success was not being replicated in the other group.

The next day someone filled me in on how things went for that group. A good friend of mine noted how he was excited that a friend of his had decided to show up—a professor of humanities at the local college. Conversation began well, and everyone was engaged in the discussion. However, the night quickly changed when someone arrived toting a stack of books, Bibles and, pamphlets under his arm. Dropping his load on to the table, the tone of the night for that group's discussion was suddenly changed.

I asked why that was. "He had arrived to tell us what he knew, not to engage in honest, open conversation." My friend went on to tell me that the rest of the evening proved that out, as every promising line of discussion was shut down by this well-meaning Christian, who clearly did not come to learn anything, but to teach the group what he knew. Apparently that was quite a lot. To emphasize his authoritative knowledge, he sat with his hand on his stack of books and Bibles, and spoke condescendingly from his throne at the end of the table. My friend was sincerely disappointed in how the evening turned out, and noted that his professor friend had to leave because it was so intolerable. This particular evening happened a couple of years ago, and as far as I know, the professor has never come back. So much for our good night.

When I reflected on the evening, I wondered how my own table could have had such a great evening of conversation, despite the diversity in make-up of the group. Many at our table cited it as "a great experience" and that they were so glad they found such an open and honest group.

Two tables, two entirely different experiences. When such things happen, I wince, because a great opportunity seems to have gone by the wayside. A unique opportunity for the group to learn, to hear a broad variety of perspectives, and to hear some thoughts from a local professor who was present that night. Yet this opportunity evaporated because of one person who felt the need to keep opening his mouth because he had nothing to learn. He felt he already had all the answers. (This is not to pick on a Christian, as we have had an evening with a similarly obnoxious atheist.)

This scenario has played out more than once, though overall it has been rare. It is actually surprising to me that this doesn't happen more often. Where do these folks come from with this kind of attitude? The same place I do. A place where we know we have the answers to all the major questions about God and life, and that the real struggle is not in learning anything new so much as in convincing everyone else how right we are. A place that makes us—let alone the gospel—seem awfully unattractive. We can do better than that. If we want to see more of the kingdom of God unfolding in our midst, it may not be optional.

5

The Art of Listening

The first service that one owes to others
in the fellowship
consists of listening to them.
Just as love of God begins with listening to his word,
so the beginning of love for our brothers and sisters
is learning to listen to them.

— Dietrich Bonhoeffer, *Life Together*

I've heard it said there's a window
that opens from one mind to another.
But if there's no wall,
there's no need for fitting the window,
or the latch.

— Jalal Al-din Rumi

AN EXPLOSIVE COCKTAIL

It was a pleasant vacation up until that point. My family and I were vacationing at a cabin in the woods in Michigan. A little place on twenty acres with plenty of solitude, and a lot to commend it for a quiet retreat. In fact, part of this book has been written at this very spot. On this particular occasion my wife and kids and I were camping with my extended family: a summer getaway. Everyone was there: my parents, my sister and her family, and my brother and his family. It was the first such extended-family vacation we'd had in years. Between walks in the woods, competitive games of horseshoes, water balloon fights, and smores over the campfire, we were having a great time.

But one topic of conversation would change all of that in a hurry. Politics. This was during the summer before the 2008 election. My wife and I, as many others, had become disillusioned with the path our country had taken under the previous administration. Numerous wars under the pretext of "spreading freedom" or "fighting terrorism" had led us in a difficult spot, not only in regard to our standing in the world, but in terms of a debt that continued to balloon under unlimited spending by the defense department. We happened to voice that we were intrigued by other candidates (i.e., non-Republicans).

"But Obama wants universal health care!"

"And Hillary, well, she's married to Bill."

"And Obama is a socialist."

We should have kept our mouths shut, but somehow we couldn't. My wife responded.

"Actually I think universal health care could be a good thing."

"What are you talking about? That's socialism. I'm not paying a dime for someone who hasn't earned the right to have it on their own."

"Yeah, and who's going to pay for that?"

"Well, we seem to be finding plenty of money to spend on killing people in other countries—perhaps we could divert some of those resources toward healing people in our own."

"Are you serious? What's going on? You sound like a Democrat, or worse."

I can't remember what else went on in that conversation, other than that my wife and I were viewed with suspicion from that time forward. How could we dare to think differently? Yet in all honesty, we got the response we deserved.

I look back at that conversation with a fair amount of regret. I had some newfound views on politics and even faith, but was not prepared to share them in a tactful way. What was meant as genuine excitement was instead uttered as an attack, and I found myself opposing, even ridiculing, positions I had formerly held—and they still did. One of the things I have learned since that time, over conversations with others of differing view points, is that being loud, being dismissive, using stereotypes, and being aggressive are all terribly ineffective ways to communicate, and often have the opposite effect than was intended. It serves to alienate rather than draw in. Looking back, I don't blame my family for their responses. I had earned it.

Be honest. You've had an experience like this as well, where in one conversation a person goes from a trusted friend or family member to someone who was under suspicion. It is amazing how quickly we can turn someone we disagree with into the "other." If this can happen in a family, or with a good friend, how much more might it happen in a setting at the bar, with strangers—over beer?!

Such an explosion is a possibility every Thursday night. Rabbi Brad Hirschfield has noted that "all passions are like fire; they can warm your house, or burn it down with you in it." Sounds dangerous. He notes that this includes: "religious, political, and familial passions."[1] He's exactly right. When we're dealing with things that are at the core of who we are, things that we hold dearly, things that affect the very lens through which we see the world—even the lens itself!—we can be a bit testy, a bit defensive, a bit protective of our territory. After all, our thoughts in many ways construct the world we live in, and we tend to like where we live. When someone threatens that, we act accordingly.

So how does one avoid this? What do we do to keep the recipe of religion, politics, God, and alcohol from becoming an exploding Molotov cocktail? Perhaps we've been lucky. Or had some divine protection. We certainly have asked for trouble. Maybe we're just a calm bunch in Northern Michigan—we just drove through twelve inches of snow to get here, we're not going to show up and turn on each other. But I think it's more than that.

EVERYONE WHO ASKS

Pub Theology began with the simple premise of listening before speaking. Despite beginning with this in mind at the outset, what I and others from

---

1. From a lecture given June 6, 2010 at Trinity United Church of Christ, Northport, Michigan.

my community found was that the biggest challenge for us, particularly those of us from a more evangelical Christian position, was learning to keep our mouths shut. We are bred to "always have an answer to everyone who asks," and when all else fails, the answer is—you guessed it—Jesus. But we found out quickly that that doesn't really play very well when you're dealing with people who have already been through that routine and found it wanting.

What we discovered is that, rather than having an answer to everyone who asks, better to be those who ask. Asking questions are absolutely crucial to the process of listening. When someone makes a statement I disagree with, my natural response is to quickly correct them, or provide reason X, Y, and Z as to why they are wrong. I have learned through conversations and Facebook discussions gone bad (I know you've been there too!) that such an approach is very seldom profitable. What does help, however, is repeating someone's statement, followed up by, "Did I hear you correctly?" This affirms to them that you actually heard what they said. After a person is affirmed in such a way, he or she will often be relieved to know that they have not unwittingly entered into a debate or a shouting match. Someone has taken the time to hear one's concern or perspective. This sets the tone of the conversation dial to "mutual" or "friendly," rather than "combative" or "hostile." This is not easy. And given the nature of the topics at Pub Theology, it is a learned behavior. Even an art.

As I noted at the outside of this chapter, this does not come naturally to me at all. Listening is hard work. If it was easy, everyone would do it.

TO HELL WITH JESUS

One particular evening, we were discussing Peter Rollins' parable entitled: "The Last Trial." It goes like this:

> You sit in silence contemplating what has just taken place. Only moments ago you were alive and well, relaxing at home with friends. Then there was a deep, crushing pain in your chest that brought you crashing to the floor. The pain has now gone, but you are no longer in your home. Instead, you find yourself standing on the other side of death waiting to stand before the judgment seat and discover where you will spend eternity. As you reflect upon your life your name is called, and you are led down a long corridor into a majestic sanctuary with a throne located in its center. Sitting

on this throne is a huge, breathtaking being who looks up at you and begins to speak.

"My name is Lucifer, and I am the angel of light."

You are immediately filled with fear and trembling as you realize that you are face to face with the enemy of all that is true and good. Then the angel continues: "I have cast God down from his throne and banished Christ to the realm of eternal death. It is I who hold the keys to the kingdom. It is I who am the gatekeeper of paradise, and it is for me alone to decide who shall enter eternal joy and who shall be forsaken."

After saying these words, he sits up and stretches out his vast arms. "In my right hand I hold eternal life and in my left eternal death. Those who would bow down and acknowledge me as their god shall pass through the gates of paradise and experience an eternity of bliss, but all those who refuse will be vanquished to the second death with their Christ."

After a long pause, he bends toward you and speaks, "Which will you choose?"[2]

The question before us, given the above scenario, was: would you choose paradise with Satan or hell with Jesus? There were differing opinions, and two women who had arrived together disagreed and nearly came to blows over it:

"I would go to hell with Jesus."

"No you wouldn't."

"I would."

"What? Of course you wouldn't! *No one* would! You'd choose heaven."

At this point, someone stepped in. "You say you'd go to hell with Jesus? Why is that?"

"Well, I think that he is the one I'm after, and that is more important to me than the stuff that comes along with it."

The questioner responded: "I'd like to think I'd do the same, but I'm not sure." Then the other woman was addressed: "Why do you think most people would choose heaven over Jesus?"

"It seems to me that people of faith are mostly in it for the payoff after they die."

What was unfolding as a possible argument shifted into a compelling conversation. This clever parable was causing a few of us to rethink what our motives were in following Jesus. Why do we follow Jesus? Because of

2. Rollins, *Orthodox Heretic*, 87

the payoff? So we don't go to hell when we die? Because we think it's true? Because we grew up with it? Because we think its the best way to live?

After the conversation continued along these lines for awhile, one person present asked this challenging question: "If I think I would choose hell in this scenario, do I choose to find Jesus in the hells of this world?"

This was an engaging conversation, both for the people of faith as well as the non-believers present. A conversation that was allowed to flourish because someone was willing to listen.

SHOOT FIRST, ASK QUESTIONS LATER

"Love what you're doing," wrote one elderly gentleman who heard about our gatherings. "Back in the eighties we used to do things just like that— we'd invite unbelievers to our church for lectures and then afterward have a Q & A time." Notice the pattern: speak first, then, if there's time, listen.

I similarly read about a college group doing what they called Theology on Tap (or something similar) on their campus. The gathering met in a lecture hall and had scheduled speakers for each evening. After the speaker spoke on a particular topic, they would then open up a time for questions. A great idea—and certainly we desperately need settings where experts can come and teach us. But again, notice the pattern: speak first, then listen (if there's time). It's not as open as it appears. Attendees are invited primarily to sit and listen to someone else's perspective.

Our goal was not to create a program that we run where we give our perspective and then allow questions, time permitting. From the outset we wanted to make sure that this was not going to be a "setup." In other words, get people in the door, "pretend" to have a conversation, then hit them up for a gospel presentation. Rather, we wanted to allow anyone and everyone to come and give their perspective. To share their story. To unload their baggage about religion, about faith, about God. To have a group that is willing to listen without judgment, to accept without demanding conformity, to simply embrace them as another human being, which is to say, a person with yearnings that some would call spiritual or religious or, as my humanist friends might say, wonder and awe at the universe.

I remember attempting to explain this approach to a friend. That our goal at this gathering was first and foremost to listen.

"Why would you do that?"

"So I can get to know them. Learn about them. Discover what they think and believe, and begin to understand where they are coming from."

"Who cares what they think? Just give 'em the Bible!"

STARS UPON THARS

Within my experiences of Christianity, predominantly in Reformed and evangelical circles, we constantly feel that we need to be out telling others the "Truth" (with a capital "T")—whether it is salvation in four easy steps, or an incomprehensible doctrine of predestination. What effect does this attitude have on our disposition toward outsiders? Superiority. We have the answers, you have the questions. We have the knowledge, you have the ignorance. We are the teachers, you are the students. I cannot tell you how thoroughly this attitude has permeated so much of Western Christianity, and the night at the pub that we highlighted last chapter saw it play out to its logical conclusion.

We unwittingly do this to ourselves when we claim to have the corner on divinely infallible and unquestionable truth. This is IT! How can we not share it? How can we not have an air of superiority—we've figured it out. Hallelujah, hand me the tracts, and let me find someone to be the victim of my newfound certainty. Rarely do we pause and think about how this attitude might be perceived by those we approach, nor do we consider the fact that we may not actually have the "truth" as completely and accurately as we assume.

It is natural to surround ourselves with like-minded people. Yet by doing this, our assumptions and presuppositions are rarely, if ever, challenged or questioned. And even though we are dimly aware that others don't think the way we do—their perspective is quickly written off as we make it our main agenda to convert them to our way of seeing things, or failing that, simply label them "the lost" or "godless," and therefore "wrong," and with nothing to offer us. A lack of interaction with people who think differently can lead to an underlying naïveté that the reason such persons think the way they do is simply because they've never accurately been presented with the gospel. We can easily become like the Sneetches of Dr. Seuss fame, who assume that only those who have stars upon thars are worth anything. And the star is, of course, Jesus. And so our response to people who have genuine questions, or who legitimately believe something else often goes like this:

"You don't believe in God? Have you ever heard of Jesus?"

"You wonder how a good God created a world in which evil exists? That is a good question. But the real question is: what are you going to do about the evil in your heart?"

Those are not necessarily bad approaches, but they fail to give much respect to the person one is engaging. We were determined to break out of the routine where people show up with genuine and hard questions, and we simply respond with well-meaning, but ultimately unsatisfying, Sunday school answers. We didn't want it to be a scenario that promoted 'open conversation', when in fact we planned no such thing.

Some approached our gathering with genuine trepidation, fearing that they were walking into the newest and hippest evangelism effort. Steve, now a regular on Thursday nights, noted having this exact fear. "I was afraid this would be another place where answers took priority over questions, and where only Christian answers were welcome." He was worried this was just a guise for recruiting new converts, where we'd slap a Jesus sticker on unsuspecting attendees, like Sylvester McMonkey McBean's star-on, star-off machine. What effect did this have on his participation? "I initially failed to reveal that I'm an atheist, because in most settings people would be so busy trying to convert me that they wouldn't bother listening to what I was saying." And then, in a revelation that hit all too close to home, he noted: "In most settings I've been in, telling people you are an atheist causes them to automatically lose respect for you."

It was very sobering, not to mention saddening, to hear that. Our goal at Pub Theology was to have a genuine conversation, whether or not you had a star on your belly, or on your backside, on your forearm, or whether you'd never even heard of stars. There was no prerequisite to sit at the table, simply a desire to learn from others, and engage in honest conversation. And so it was not without a small sense of humble gratitude that I heard Steve add: "I quickly found out that this group wasn't like that." We had set out to create a setting of listening and respect. Perhaps in some small way we were succeeding.

The question remains: How do you prevent the conversation from being hijacked by people who arrive intending to preach? This really is a good question, and we have had atheists as well as Christians come with such an agenda.

I recall a one such evening in particular. We were gathering at our table, and welcomed a couple who were attending for the first time. She was very soft-spoken. He was not. As soon as a young woman at the table mentioned something about her beliefs, he nearly exploded. "How can you believe that?" he spurted out in response. "Only an idiot would believe in a God who clearly doesn't exist, or if he does, obviously doesn't care or have the power to act in our world." His attitude was condescending, and he had a very hard time listening to anyone without interjecting a derogatory remark or a sigh of disgust. Atheists can be as unwilling to listen as anyone. Such lack of patience or empathy can exist in a person regardless of whether they believe in God.

We've already described what it was like when one particular fundamentalist Christian arrived bringing a stack of books, Bibles, and tracts. He apparently thought he was going to be called upon to give a sermon or theological lecture, or invited to hand out tracts to everyone. He was at the wrong meeting. He dominated the discussion and those at his table felt helpless as the conversation was hijacked. When such a person shows up, we subtly encourage them to realize that they aren't at a forum where we are all going to close our eyes, pray, and have the opportunity to raise a hand for Jesus at the end. It isn't going to happen. There may well be a time and place for creating such an atmosphere, but this one is not it.

I am glad to say that people such as this particular Christian and the afore-mentioned atheist have actually been in the minority at our gatherings. When those people do come, we attempt to ask questions in response and not take their vehemence personally. I'd like to say we always succeed in staying patient and respectful, but no doubt we haven't done it perfectly. Such a hostile approach can affect everyone, making it difficult to maintain an environment of respect and dialogue, despite our best attempts.

TAKING A SEAT

When we first began our meetings at the pub, I remember being asked by several people, "So, do you teach people at the pub?" Upon my answering in the negative, they quickly said, "But you give the answers or teach a lesson at the end, right?" It remains hard for many to grasp that we are seeking a truly open discussion, where the atheist or the Marxist or the Muslim could have the floor (or even—gasp!—the final say) as much as anyone else. While the approach of "let me teach you" is certainly appropriate in many settings, in a setting that is seeking truly open dialogue, it is inappropriate and out of place. Rabbi Brad Hirschfield has said that before we can become someone's teacher, we must become his or her student. Hirschfield notes that "if you listen long enough to someone's beliefs, they will become curious about yours, and that is half the battle."[3] If we can move from the place of power—the place that seeks to enforce its views on others, to the place of humility—the place that seeks to learn from others, we just might learn something, and yes, even have something to impart.

Listening. It's an art. And it's awfully hard work. Yet these opportunities to learn—as well as to share—are all around us. Christianity in the West has for so long assumed that it has everything to give and nothing to learn. We have taken the role again and again of teacher and preacher. We have talked loud and often, seeking to control the conversation, and manipulate the discussion to our own ends. It's time for us to take a seat in the classroom, to pull up a chair at the table, and listen.

3. Hirschfield, in a talk delivered at Trinity United Church of Christ, Northport, MI on June 6, 2010.

6

An (Un)Safe Place

The opposite of control is celebration . . .

—Matthew Fox

CONTROL FREAKS

It is easy to talk about listening. Yet even once we understand its importance, we often fail to do it. A friend of mine involved in a campus ministry heard about our Pub Theology gatherings. As I shared with him some of the diversity of the crowd that gathered, he began to think of ways they could creatively engage non-Christians on their campus as well. He decided to hold a "Skeptics' Questions Night." He ran the idea by his group and everyone felt it was a great idea. They decided to go for it. They set up the night, put up posters, and invited the campus freethinkers' club as well as a philosophy professor. I was not able to attend but was able to listen to a recording of the event online. I tuned in with enthusiasm and an expectation of some very good questions coming from some atheists, freethinkers, and professors.

I wondered how my friend and his group would handle some of these questions. How would the discussion go? My friend opened the evening with some welcoming statements, after which I assumed there would be an open mic and some questions (it was a large group gathering, so not exactly a gather-round-a-table event). However, my friend kept speaking. And I realized he had prepared a talk for the evening about the idea of asking questions and talking with skeptics, rather than spending the evening actually engaging skeptics and their questions.

He spoke for at least an hour, and then ended the evening encouraging folks to ask questions and find people who have questions. As I listened I was somewhat surprised and began to realize that what my friend had advertised as "Skeptics' Questions Night" was actually one of their regular campus religious meetings that centered around a talk or sermon, and that it wasn't really what they had advertised. They had invited skeptics to attend and bring questions, but forgot to allow the skeptics any place or way to actually ask those questions!

The longer I listened, the more I began to feel badly for any skeptical or questioning folks that decided to attend. I found out later that the freethinkers group did not show up, and neither did the philosophy professor. I was relieved, but still felt badly for anyone who did come expecting the chance to actually ask questions. It turned out to be a very good talk my friend gave, and I told him that in my feedback. But I also said to him that to have a true skeptics' questions night, you need (a) skeptics, and (b) questions. He agreed, and I think in retrospect realized he shouldn't have titled the evening the way he did, because any skeptic who attended would have felt short-changed.[1]

As Christians, it seems we have an innate need to control the flow of information to ensure desired outcomes. (This may well be a part of the general human condition, but people of faith somehow excel at it.) Having a lecture or time of teaching on a given topic allows the coordinators of the gathering to control the agenda and to control the topic and to some extent, control the way people are supposed to think. My friend Samir Selmanovic has remarked that one critic of the church said recently, "How come you Christians never participate in things you can't control?"

Ouch. A great question. We have a very hard time with letting go— with allowing truly open-ended conversation that doesn't lead toward a nicely wrapped ending with a gospel presentation of some sort. Now there may well be a time and place for that, but non-Christians are so used to this approach that they become uninterested in getting roped

---

1. Let it also be noted that my friend remains involved in a campus ministry of the kind I was involved in during college, and does so in very thoughtful and engaging ways. In fact, recently they had a representative from the Secular Student Alliance as the featured speaker for their weekly gathering. His topic: "Why you shouldn't follow Jesus."

into yet another sales presentation, culminating in a reminder that they too can be part of the club if they only sign on the dotted line or pray a particular prayer.

Paulo Freire, the great Brazilian educator, has documented how the control of information with the air of divine sanction can keep people in oppressed cultures in their oppressed state. Such oppressed people are only allowed to absorb information through the filter of their oppressors, and are in effect told that things are exactly how God wants them.[2]

Are churches any different when they operate in more or less the same way? Are they similarly controlling? Perhaps we have created classes of oppressed people theologically. Our fear, coupled with the need to control the flow of information, causes us to endorse certain theological perspectives as being "right" (usually the ones we hold), while labeling others as "wrong," "misguided," or even "heretical." Thus theological exploration is highly discouraged, and we are only allowed to study or voice theological opinions within our own particular tradition.

I grew up feeling unbelievably blessed that I believed and understood the truth of Christianity, and not only that, but that my particular brand of it was the truest version out there. In other words, out of all the people who have ever lived in the history of the world, my particular denomination, this small group comprised by and large of former Dutch immigrants, was privileged by God over all others to have been granted the best and clearest picture of Him. But if you pause to think about it, it is an almost absurd position to hold. Yet hold it we did, and we couldn't wait for the opportunity to enlighten some other less fortunate Christian about the clarity and glories of our particular faith tradition. We would be ready to drop the books on the table, and start the lecture.

But let's pause a second. Even if you are convinced you've got such a corner on the truth, is this the best approach to getting someone to understand you? Paulo Freire has noted—in line with Rabbi Hirschfield—that the best learning happens when teachers see themselves as teacher-learners and their students as learner-teachers.[3] In other words, regardless of our position in a relationship, we need to see ourselves as needing (and able) to learn from those we are interacting with. You need to encourage and coordinate group conversation without directing it to a hidden but

2. Cited in Herzog, *Parables as Subversive Speech*, 28
3. Ibid., 20.

previously determined conclusion. In a group setting, such as a classroom (or a gathering at the pub), Freire notes that if the facilitator dominates the group, the culture circle will simply "reproduce the relations of production and power already regnant in the society and culture."[4] In other words, new ways of thinking are kept at bay.

One small way we have tried to express our own commitment to keeping the floor open is that when I am not able to be at the gathering, one of our regular attending atheists is the facilitator of the discussion. Some would be mortified to know this. (Shh! Don't tell.) He will no doubt bring different topics and questions than I would. It sets the tone that everyone is valued here, and no one's position is privileged over another. And as noted earlier, I regularly seek input on the questions and topics that I bring as discussion starters, and try to draw from many religious traditions, so that at least at a minimal level, many voices are represented at the table.

ANYTHING GOES?

So do we Christians have nothing to say? Or am I saying that all beliefs are equally true? Or is there, as one book title suggests, "no place for truth"? Some of you are reading this chapter and cringing. Everything inside you says, "But, but, but—Jesus is the only way! Make sure people get that!"

Having a truly open forum is something most Christians are afraid to do, because we want control. We want to know where the discussion is going, and where it is going to end up. You can see this in the format of most Christian approaches to evangelism such as the *Alpha Course.* There is a group discussion—which provides the impression of open dialogue— but it is all heading toward a predetermined destination. Again, this can be a great approach in many settings, but too often, it is the *only* approach.

It is not that we have nothing to say. Rather, it means we respect people enough to care about what they think, rather than pre-emptively assuming we have the answer to every question they have about life. So how do we articulate our beliefs to someone? A friend of mine described his approach in sharing his own thoughts in a simple, yet profound way: (1) acknowledge your own uncertainties; (2) seek commonalities; and (3) use influence rather than imposing power. In other words, become a fellow learner, a fellow traveler, rather than taking the presumptive position

4. Ibid., 20.

of authority on whatever point it is you are attempting to share. There is much wisdom in that simple approach.

Many of us who have spent some time at these pub discussions over the last several years have found that when we open ourselves up, we have a lot to learn! Atheists and agnostics began to show up asking questions like "Why?"

"Why is there something, rather than nothing?"

"Why is there a God at all?"

Buddhists and Hindus began to show up and share profound spiritual insights, such as seeking inner quiet and dealing with suffering. A Muslim friend shared his approach of accepting what is and submitting to the will of Allah. Religious Jews shared the power of ritual and festival, and secular Jews articulated how one can have a deep-rooted sense of tradition and the meaning of God, without actually having to believe in God in the traditional sense.

If anyone's immediate response to such folks was to point out all the ways we disagree, they likely would not have stayed, and certainly we would have all missed an opportunity for growth.

AN (UN)SAFE PLACE

Having an attitude of listening and learning is not just a clever, back-handed approach to still getting what I want—it is about being genuine. A reason fewer and fewer people are showing up at church may well be that no one there seems to listen. Creating a truly "safe" space, where someone can express their doubts (God forbid—even the pastor!), their beliefs, their hopes, and their struggles, is too rare a thing. Rebecca, a regular at our gatherings, is a former Christian who openly declares her lack of belief in God. She has noted that Pub Theology feels like a "safe place" to talk about matters of faith. She also says she never senses a tone of condescension. "So often you try to talk to people about this stuff and it's clear they feel superior to you and are less than subtle about their underlying agenda to convert you to their position," she said. "I am glad this place is different."

Some people fear that creating such an environment opens the door to people doubting or questioning their faith. Yes it does! In that sense, Pub Theology seeks to be an "unsafe place." Your thinking *will* be challenged—as it should! If one believes that he or she holds "the truth," or even, "the Truth," it ought to be able to stand up under scrutiny. If it cannot, perhaps it is not worth holding. When a person has the attitude that he should not question his belief structure, it reveals the reality that he does not actually want to know the truth, if the truth turns out to be somewhat different than the truth as he now understands it. This person wants to continue on unimpeded in his serene, but simplistic, understanding of life, God, and faith, and doesn't want to be on a boat that encounters some waves.

I understand the fear that accompanies having your beliefs challenged, and why many go out of their way to avoid such challenges. There's a question I sometimes ask (or want to ask) a person who exhibits this fear: *Is this really faith?* When you know without a doubt that you have all the right answers, and that you know the "Truth" beyond the shadow of a doubt, faith is rendered somewhat irrelevant, isn't it? Who needs faith when there is no room for doubt? It seems to me that faith comes into play when we're not quite sure, but we go ahead and trust anyway. When there is a bit of uncertainty—that is when faith has the opportunity to express itself and grow (see Chapter 10).

Some also fear that creating such an environment means that you have to agree with every perspective, or that you're not allowed to say what you really think. This is not true. It simply means that you posture yourself as a learner and listener first, and as a teacher second. It means you grant respect to the person across the table, and haven't already beforehand written their perspective off as wrong and needing to be corrected. It means setting aside an agenda to convert, and learning to converse. At that point, in humility, genuine conversation actually requires that you state what you really think, just as you expected the other person to. And when you express it as "this is how I see it," rather than "this is how it is" (see Chapter 11), that seemingly minor adjustment can make all the difference. There is still a place for personal belief, for conviction, for wanting to share what one believes. But to turn the gathering we have crafted into a place where we will invite you to a particular church or ask you to sign onto a certain theological perspective would be to betray the purpose of the gathering.

There are people all around us who think differently than we do. They have something to teach us. Each and every one of them. Unfortunately our relationships with such people often only go one way. There is no give and take. We are just too eager to give, and the sad irony is that in our zeal to share Jesus as the "way, the truth, and the life," we find ourselves opposing the very way of Jesus. In the Gospels we find a Jesus who was open, welcoming, and hospitable. I'm not sure he was as dogmatic and ungracious as many of his followers have historically been, particularly toward outsiders. (And we wonder why we don't have many non-Christian friends.)

In our gatherings at the pub, we have, albeit imperfectly, sought to recapture that way, to embody that openness and hospitality. Perhaps by even having this forum, we are in a small way incarnating Jesus to others. And as we do that, it seems that he works out his ways even in us. I have seen a number of people move from their prior position of certainty and immovability to a more nuanced place of faith, and they are glad they did.

"I used to see everything in black and white," notes one Pub Theology regular. "And boy, I realize it just isn't that simple. And for that, I'm grateful."

Another person said, "I've learned so much from the people around this table that I previously thought had nothing to teach me."

When I see this happening, particularly among those who were immersed in the culture of certainty, I know there is hope for everyone else as well. The shift is not easy, but it is worth it. It reminds me a bit of the television show *Fringe*. An updated version of *The X-Files*, it contains plenty of bizarre happenings, mind-blowing events, and even parallel universes. The FBI has a "Fringe Division" team that takes on these strange cases, much like Agents Scully and Mulder of paranormal police-work past. A new member, Agent Lincoln Lee, joins the team at some point. As he encounters one strange happening after another, he struggles to grapple with all the things that are blowing his formerly settled view of the world apart. A recent episode shows Agent Lee at a coffee shop at three in the morning confiding in a friend, "I used to believe, just a few months ago, that I understood the world we lived in. There were basic truths that I thought were . . . well true. I used to sleep like a baby, [in] blissful ignorance."[5]

It can be frightening to engage in conversations where our own "basic truths" might be challenged. It requires a place that is, by turns, both safe and unsafe. If blissful ignorance is your preference, I completely understand. But you may want to stop reading and give this book to someone else.

5. *Fringe*, Season 4, Episode 7: "Wallflower"

7

Unfiltered

"What is more edifying than light?"
"Conversation."
(So) comes the answer in Goethe's fairy tale.
But this is true only of certain special conversations which,
aiming beyond words at wordless understanding,
rest on such an understanding or "harmony" in the sphere beyond words.

—Georg Kühlewind, *Becoming Aware of the Logos*

So what do our conversations look like? Grab a beer (preferably some-thing brewed locally) and pull up a seat. In this chapter we're going to get an unfiltered (what else?) glimpse of the kinds of conversation that occur at our Pub Theology gatherings. Things to look for: diversity of opinions, moments of listening, moments of honest disagreement, places where we fail to listen, and perhaps an insight or two. Ready? Let's go.

THE SAME OLD?

The first question on the sheet that night was: "Is anything really new?" Here's how the conversation went:

> David: Yes, this experience, this moment, these people, this is new.
>
> Bryan: Explain what you mean by that.

David: Well, I've sat and had a beer with people before. Even some of you. But not this particular moment, with this exact group—some of you I'm just meeting for the first time today. That is new. This exact moment is new.

A few nods of agreement are seen around the table.

Ben: I tend to disagree. Not much is actually new. It's just the same thing in a different configuration. Consider humanity—we aren't so much different morally and otherwise than we were 2,000 years ago. We keep repeating the same mistakes and mistreating one another in similar fashion, we just may have some different ways of doing it.

Bryan: So you're saying that just as people in ancient times used to take advantage of each other, seek their own well-being and power, and so on, is more or less how we operate today?

Ben: Yes, more or less. I mean ancient Rome would go in and take over nations to use up their resources and enslave their people. Is it much different regarding nations today, even our own?

Steve: Hold on a moment. Nobody on the street today in a Western nation believes that slavery is OK. Slavery was common practice in the ancient world, and today we've moved beyond that. I would say that is a new development. So in answer to the question, that is something that is genuinely new. We have evolved ethically.

Rachel: Hmmm . . . Actually, there are more slaves today than at any other time in history.

Steve: Well, it's not quite the same thing.

Rachel: How so?

Steve: There may be a lot of slavery, but it's not exactly the same as in the past, and they have to work a lot harder to hide it, because it is conventional wisdom that slavery is not OK, that it is not morally permissible.

Bryan: OK, OK. Let's figure this out. I agree with a couple things going on here. On the one hand, Steve is right. Ask anyone on the street today about slavery—there's universal agreement that it's not OK to own another person as property. Yet I also agree with Rachel, that there is as much or more slavery happening now—via Third World factories, the sex trade, etc.—than there ever has been. How do these things both make sense?

. Steve: Well, because it is so universally condemned, in many ways it is easier to have it happen because we assume it isn't happening.

Bryan: But if we all agree that it is happening, isn't Ben right? We actually aren't that much improved or that much different morally than say, 2,000 years ago.

Steve: I don't think so. The awareness of it is something that is huge—we have taken steps to reduce slavery as something that can happen out in the open, and the fact that it still happens so much is partly due to our increased awareness of everything happening in the world, due to global communications, which in the past, was an impossibility—you knew mostly what was happening in your own neighborhood, maybe your own kingdom or nation. Also, look at the ways we treat women today, our improved concern for health and so on.

Ben: But what about wars? We continue to kill one another somewhat barbarically, even if it doesn't seem so because it's happening far away or via drones or what-have-you.

Steve: When is the last time someone invaded your neighborhood?

Bryan: Maybe we are protected—but it's called, having the largest military power in the world today. The rest of the world doesn't have the same experience.

Dave: I still posit that this moment happening right now is new.

Grins appear around the table, followed by sips of beer.

CAN GOD CHANGE THE PAST?

Following this interchange, we moved on to another question: "Can God change the past?"

Steve: I love this question.

Bryan: That's because it's your question.

Chris: What made you ask this question?

Steve: Well, I think it brings up some interesting possibilities about God and his power and his ability to make a difference in the world. I read about a man who prayed a prayer about his friends who died under awful circumstances, and he prayed that God would go back and change the past—not that he would make the accident not happen—because that would change too many future contingencies, but that he would simply remove their suffering. It wouldn't affect anyone else outside or change anything else, it would simply make their pain go away, and that was what he prayed.

David: I am often asked to pray for so and so who is having surgery at 9:00 a.m., and sometimes I remember at 11:00 a.m. and still pray for them, and I think that is worth doing.

Chris: Yeah, if God is outside of time, it shouldn't matter, right?

David: And then I hear they come through, and I'm glad I still prayed.

Bryan: But what if the surgery was at 9, and you forgot to pray until it was over, and the person died on the table? Wouldn't you feel terrible?

David: Good question. But at the same time, I don't feel that God is waiting upon my prayer to decide whether or not to bring someone through surgery, yet I still think it matters at some level, so I pray.

Aaron: I think it might be a bad thing if God changed the past. We all have things we've gone through—many of them have been pretty hard, things we'd rather not go through again—yet those things shape us in particular ways to become the people we are today. If God were to remove all the difficult things by changing the past, would we grow? Would we have character? Would we be the kind of people he wants us to be?

A few people nod. Someone responds: Good call.

Bryan: If God could change the past, how would we know it? Let's say this building burned down and we all went up in flames with it, but God said: "Whoops, can't have that." And we are now living in an alternate future in which this didn't happen. If God could change the past, how would we even know?

Chris: There is a fundamental problem with the idea of changing the past. It is logically impossible, because it entails that something both happened and didn't happen—a contradiction.

Steve: An apparent change of the past could really just be a "move" to another possible world.

Aaron: If God is outside of time, it shouldn't matter, right?

Someone responds: Yeah, God can do whatever he wants.

Chris: Can he? The idea that God is outside of time contradicts almost everything the Hebrew Bible tells us about what God does: his interactions with people, how he changes his mind—which would be pointless if he was somehow "above it all," not to mention his interventions in natural events. That seems to be more of a Greek or philosophical view of God more than a Scriptural view.

Bill: If God changed the past, it would mean he made a mistake, or he was wrong.

Rachel: He gives us free will so that we can make our own choices.

Bradley: If God could change the past, wouldn't he change what happened at the garden? Why let things get out of control?

Rachel: But we have to have free will—otherwise what would be the point of it? I have to believe that God created us with free will because he wants people who freely choose to do the right thing, who freely choose to love him and follow him.

Steve: But let's think about the garden and creation. Let's say Adam and Eve eat the apple and do the wrong thing—God could keep changing the past until they voluntarily chose to do the right thing. And he could do this infinitely until every time people chose something voluntarily, they would do it of their own volition and it wouldn't be God coercing people.

Bryan: Good points. One struggle I have is thinking about heaven, or the new creation. How will it be possible for us to love God and always obey God there without having free will? Will we not have free will? If we don't, will it actually be real? Will we just be automatons? Or if there is free will in heaven, yet we always choose to do the right thing, in other words, if this reality really is possible—why didn't God create the world this way the first time? Why create a world in which we sin and do terrible things to each other, and then some have to spend eternity in hell as a result (according to some theological systems), when all along it is possible for God to create such a reality where we all voluntarily do the right thing and love and serve him as he wants? It's a real quandary.

Steve: Exactly. If he can do it at all, why not start out that way?

Chris: If a heaven in which people freely do what is right is possible, then God should have made this world that way. It suggests free will is not a sufficient explanation for sin.

Aaron: Perhaps he allowed us to sin, even knew we would sin, so that he could demonstrate his love for us, so that he could become one of us, and we would experience the depth of God's love for us in Christ, which wouldn't have happened or even have been necessary if sin had never occurred.

Chris: But isn't that a big price to pay, all the suffering, sin, pain, evil, to get at that end result? Would that really be worth it?

Bryan: I'm pretty sure Aquinas explains all this somewhere.

PULL UP A CHAIR

Some of you reading this are wishing you could pull up a chair—to this very conversation! You're frustrated, excited, wondering, thinking . . . The best part is that you're probably already having similar conversations; you just may be lacking the space in which a larger diversity of voices is present. Well, all it takes is a table, a few chairs, and some good beverages. But more practical tips on starting your own group later.

As you can see, our conversations sometimes meander, sometimes focus, sometimes bring us to new insights, and sometimes create more questions. (The conversation above was my best attempt to recreate the actual conversation the next day—not quite verbatim, but I think close enough to give you a taste of what was discussed.) Perhaps you can sense that the important thing happening here is not necessarily that we arrive at the answers. Answers to questions we all have are indeed important, and we should seek to answer them. But here we are not beginning with the presupposition that we already have all the answers we need. Rather, we open ourselves up to hear what each other has to say, to new possibilities, and we do so in a spirit of respect and interest. It is great if along the way a question one of us has gets answered, but this is not guaranteed. The goal here is to have different ideas and perspectives interact, intersect, and along the way—a step in our understanding of God and the world may well be taken.

The neat thing is that it is a journey that happens in community. Though you arrive with your own perspectives, you will inevitably be shaped by the varying people who are present on a given evening. What often happens is a sort of deconstruction of one's prior beliefs and understandings, which isn't necessarily a bad thing. It is important to distinguish deconstruction from destruction. As Wes Howard-Brooks notes in his introduction to his commentary on the Gospel of John, "the powerful tool known as deconstruction challenges us to dig beneath any viewpoints that claim to be 'objective' or 'foundational' for the preconceived notions and commitments that underlie them. If we believe that God calls us to break down the altars of idolatry that pose as divine centers in our society, we should also be willing to examine both our own false gods and the images of the true God that animate us."[1] As Calvin College philosophy professor James K.A. Smith notes, "Deconstruction is a work of love, and deconstruction happens because it is animated by a vision for something different."[2] In other words, deconstruction is not the end goal, but an important—and perhaps necessary—part of making sure the foundations of our beliefs are as solid as they can be. Was it Jesus who mentioned something about not building houses on improper foundations?

Compare the above Pub Theology conversations to a Bible study or church Sunday School class. In those settings, the initial discussion on morality would go a bit different. Question: what is morality, and how can we know it? Answer: Morality is that which is found in God's Word. God is the moral law-giver. But this simple question and answer—while very useful and functional—doesn't leave space for the subsequent questions that such an answer unearths. At Pub Theology, someone would likely ask: Which parts of God's Word? The parts about not cooking a goat in its mother's milk? The part where we are commended to kill everything that has breath, including women and children? The part where I am never to wear two kinds of fabric? Or is it the Sermon on the Mount? Or the Ten Commandments (and which version)?

Let's get to the second topic: "Can God change the past?" This gets to the problem of evil. Sunday School scenario: Why is there evil in the

---

1. Howard-Brooks, *Becoming Children of God*, 8.

2. Cited in Caputo, *What Would Jesus Deconstruct?*, 16

world? Answer: God allows it by giving his creatures free will. OK. Pub Theology scenario: But what about the fact that God is sovereign (all powerful)? Couldn't he prevent it without removing our free will? And how do we have free will if we also believe in the doctrine of predestination? Those things are mutually exclusive, aren't they? (At least without coming up with some theories about how the one "appears" to be true and the other is "ultimately" true). These and a dozen other subsequent questions that arise are too often stifled in the atmosphere of certainty.

The reality is that many people are tired of not being able to be honest, and it is likely their integrity rather than their depravity that keeps them from being a part of a church community. They've had it with simple answers and being told what to think and how to think it. The world is not simple, and questions of life and faith and God—theological questions—are profoundly complex. The illusion is that there is a set of answers that deals with all of these challenges or that we're not allowed to continue to develop our understanding of God because all the answers are to be found in a book by our favorite theologian(s). This is simply unsatisfying for many people today, including me.

I asked one fellow who attends our Thursday evening sessions fairly often but who does not attend church: "Why don't you attend church?"

Taking a sip from his pint glass, he looked at me and said, "This is my church."

Indeed. It has congregants, talk of God, spirits, and yes—even a pew. Sound good? Grab a pint and pull up a chair.

8

The Bible Over a Beer

The Bible is true,
and some things happened . . .
It is a mistake to look to the Bible to close a discussion;
the Bible seeks to open one.

—William Sloan Coffin, *Credo*

Beware the man of one book.

—St. Thomas Aquinas

THE GOOD BOOK

During worship gatherings of my own faith community, we often have dialogue as part of the preaching. At a recent gathering, I asked the question: "How do we know when someone in authority is acting unjustly, or when a law or system is unjust?" Someone answered, "We have to test everything against the Word of God. That's our guide of absolute truth."

Now on the one hand, as a Christian whose faith is shaped and grounded in those Scriptures, I resonate with that comment. On the other hand, when I hear it put so simply, as if all we have to do is open the Good Book and the answers will fall in our lap, I want to cringe. So in that particular service I was grateful when someone else countered (before I had a chance to) by saying, "People in positions of authority have used the Word of God as their 'absolute' guide and done horrible things."

Discussion. Dialogue. Pub Theology on a Sunday morning. I was grateful for that response, and am glad to be in a community where participation is the norm, and can't help but feel that our evenings at the pub have helped deepen our faith.

Let's go back to that initial comment for a moment. A simple statement made from a place of faith: "We have to test everything against the Word of God. That's our guide of absolute truth." Fair enough. Sounds, on the face of it, like the "right" answer. But you can see how such an approach can also be dangerous. The reality is that the Bible has been used to authorize horrendous actions throughout history. It has also fostered many wonderful and selfless actions. To simply say, "The Bible says so," may be appropriate in the faith of a child, but is such an unnuanced approach appropriate for an adult? As a Christian who seeks dialogue with people of various perspectives, is it OK to just "give 'em the Bible"?

Some folks show up to Pub Theology with the Bible in one hand and beer in the other, and in many ways I don't blame them. They want to be able to defer to their document of faith if the conversation allows. Generally I do not bring a Bible to the pub, or if I do, it stays in my bag and off the table. Why? Am I ashamed of the Bible? Am I unwilling to use the Scriptures to point out who and what I think God is, and what he is like?

No. The reason I don't bring a Bible and set it on the table is that too often what this communicates to others at the table is, "It's OK to have an 'open' discussion, but don't forget I've got this heavy book over here that will trump whatever you have to say, and I'm not afraid to use it!" Because we want to foster a setting of invitation and open discussion, where all perspectives are welcome, it's just not helpful to have a big Bible sitting on the table. The reality is, if we need to check out a verse or read a chapter, anyone at the table can access the Bible on their phones, or failing that, someone may have one in a bag. It's a minor thing, and you may well have a different approach. But when entering potentially volatile situations, minor things really matter!

TAKING THE BIBLE SERIOUSLY

The question we need to assess here is this: "What is the Bible?" We have asked that at pub gatherings in the past. Here's a sampling of the responses:

"An old book of folklore."

"The Word of God."

"A collection of ancient writings."

"A bunch of fairy tales and myths that no thinking adult believes anymore."

"The inerrant Word of God."

"A holy book."

Even these responses help you see that it is not as simple as "giving 'em the Bible." If people don't hold a certain level of belief concerning what the Bible is, simply pulling it out and quoting some verses will have about as much effect as pulling out Lewis Carroll's Through the Looking Glass and attempting to convince everyone present that there really are talking rabbits. So how, as a person of faith, and faith in the God of the Bible, should one understand the Bible, and attempt to refer to it as a resource in such a setting?

This is a critical question, and I think it deserves a whole chapter. Actually it deserves a whole book. (See the Recommended Reading appendix for further resources.) At the outset, I think it is important to acknowledge that unnuanced, uncritical, one might even say naïve approaches to the Bible have helped strip it of the respect it once held in our culture.

As a Christian, I don't deny that the Bible is our guide in matters of faith and that it teaches us many truths about God. The problem is the attitude that the Bible can be put on the table to end discussion. That the Bible is so clear in its message that all we have to do is open it and submit to it. This is simply a poor and inaccurate view of what the Bible is. If it is so simple, clear-cut, and obvious, we have to ask: why is there such a myriad of interpretations of various passages, not to mention various religions spawned from it, and within those religions, endless variations and denominations?

I've found that studying the Bible with those of other faiths or no faith allows me to see it in a new light. It has slowly dawned on me in my own studies and in conversations with others that the reality, as usual, is a bit more complex. The Bible—or we might say, each book within the

Bible—was written by a particular community of faith, for a particular community of faith. It was written in history, by human beings, each and every one of whom had their own agenda, bias, and perspective. Does that mean it is not from God? Not at all. But it does mean that its message is not always going to be clear, unified, and simple. There are texts that don't just appear contradictory—they are contradictory! For those with a simplistic view of the Bible, this is a problem (that some go to great lengths to explain away). But for those who see the Bible as voicing the experiences of people who have encountered God throughout history in a diversity of ways and over hundreds and thousands of years, it should be expected. If the Bible was obvious and simple to understand, I wouldn't have a job (and my seminary training would have been a waste of time and money). It is anything but simple. It is a complex piece of literature, which defies easy classification and interpretation, partially because it is really a collection of books rather than a single book.

The reality is, I love the Bible—it's my favorite book in the whole world—and I think it has impacted our world more than any other book, and I think it continues to speak powerfully today. And if it is such an important book, an avenue through which we access the divine, then we ought to take it that seriously. Taking it seriously does not mean we just simply say, "There it is—God's Word! If it says, 'Jump!' we'll jump." That might appear on the surface to be taking it seriously, but it is also a bit naïve (taking it literally is not the only way to take it seriously).

It is actually more respectful to the Bible to care it about it so much that you are willing to take it on its own terms, as an ancient text, as something that was written in a particular historical setting, in a particular language and in a specific context. And if I really care about the Bible like I say I do, then I ought to invest all the time, energy, and resources I have available to dive into that historical setting: What was happening elsewhere in the ancient world? How might other cultures have affected what was going on when this was written? What do we know about the author or authors, if anything? Was this particular text written by a people in power, or a people under oppression? What language was this written in? What nuances are we missing when we just read it in English? What impact does the cultural context have on this text? Would an Eastern person in ancient times perhaps read this differently than a (post)modern, post-Enlightenment Westerner? What difference does my own place, history, and tradition make when I approach the text? To ignore all this and say you are taking the Bible seriously is simply inaccurate. (Maybe well intended, but false.) While we can never recover all the complexities of a past historical context (ask a historian!), we can go a long way toward gathering information that helps us along the path.

When someone shows up at a pub theology discussion and drops a heavy Bible on to the table, it seems to accompany an attitude of: "This is the end of the discussion. If we have questions—we can just open this up and find the answers." But the reality is, more often than not, opening the Bible will result in more questions! And this should not be a problem if we view the Bible as a communal document, written for community, to be discussed, studied, and learned in community (recall the afore-mentioned worship service).

Again, this is a perspective I have gained from my Jewish friends, who note that the Torah should never be studied in isolation, but in community. One should always study with a study partner, or havruta. Will Willimon, former professor at Duke Divinity School, and longtime dean of the Duke University Chapel, notes that "the Bible is the product of the believing community, and it is meant to be read in community. Solitary reading of Scripture has gotten us into all manner of difficulties."[1]

What I love about our gatherings at the Pub is that even though it is not a Bible study where I'm going to have a strong spiritual experience with like-minded believers, I know that I'm going to have my own faith challenged and pressed. And when my faith is pressed, it is going to force me to take it that much more seriously, to look that much more intently at what it is I believe.

Some fear that this perspective takes away from the Bible's divine in-spiration (or the work of the Holy Spirit). But perhaps the converse is true. Here we have to acknowledge the limitations that an academic pursuit of the text provides us. There is a point at which the scholars of history and language can only take us so far. At some point, we need to allow the text to engage us, rather than vice versa. If people truly were experiencing God as they wrote these words, if they were having a genuine encounter with the divine, would we expect everything to come out orderly? Would everything line up properly and make perfect sense when God himself shows up? Is it not precisely the poetics of the text, the jumbled narratives,

1. Conder and Rhodes, *Free for All*, back cover endorsement.

the varied descriptions of the same event that are some times at odds that give evidence not of its humanness, but of its divinity?

Peter Rollins, a philosopher and theologian from Belfast, notes as much: "God's Word is thus testified to indirectly by the parallactical nature of the text itself, being communicated by the rich, weaving web of wounded words that testify to the happening of a divine event."[2] In other words, the Bible is such a rich and powerful book, not because it all makes sense or is easy to understand, but precisely the opposite—because it continues to surprise, to evoke something deep within its readers who approach it in a state of seeking, and as such, it continues to be a deep source of mystery and meaning.

SEVENTY FACES

In my first preaching class in seminary I was given the Parable of the Soils as my first preaching text. The beauty of preaching class is that you get a bunch of students who write sermons and then "preach" them to each other in class. Awkward! I had been dreading this part of seminary, as speaking in front of people was not my cup of tea. At the same time, I was excited about the text I had received. How hard could it be to preach on a parable?

I investigated various sources, commentaries, rabbinical sources, whatever I could find. The approach I decided to focus on was that Jesus was speaking to people as those who receive the Word—those who need to examine what kind of soil they are: hard soil, rocky soil, thorny soil—all of which are inhospitable to what is sown—or soft soil in which the seed of the Word can take root. My sermon examined the various things in life that can "crowd out" and "choke" the word God is speaking to us, and how "the desire for other things" can sometimes lead to our forgetting about God and how he is calling us to live. This is probably the way the parable is most often read and understood, so I wasn't breaking any new ground here.

Despite my nerves, I managed to preach the sermon and then handed it in to my seventy year old, soon-to-retire preaching professor. He had written a textbook on preaching that was entitled, The Modern Preacher and the Ancient Text. We used to joke that, given his age, it should have been entitled, The Ancient Preacher and the Modern Text.

---

2. Rollins, *The Fidelity of Betrayal*, 57.

He was a professor who we had a lot of respect for—he had heard more sermons than we would ever preach.

I was nervous, knowing I could have done a better job, not only of studying the text, but of crafting a message which made the text alive and relevant. I took my seat, ready to take my lumps. My classmates were mostly generous, giving some constructive criticism and helpful feedback. What I was not expecting was my professor to tell me that I "got the text wrong." How could I "get it wrong?" What does that mean? This isn't Sunday School, where there are clearly delineated right and wrong answers, is it? I had assumed this was graduate school for theology. What was my professor talking about—I got the text wrong?

My professor was operating out of the old preaching handbook that states that every text has one, and only one, correct interpretation. Apparently he had insight to this one correct meaning of which I was obviously unaware. The right interpretation, I was to learn, was that Jesus was preparing the disciples for the various responses they would get to their own preaching. Apparently it was a teaching for the teachers, rather than a sermon to the gathered masses. That did make a certain amount of sense. How could I have missed it?

I took my poor grade on the sermon, and thought about getting out of the preaching business right then and there. (There are some Sundays where I still wish I had!) But my initial thought was, "Couldn't Jesus be doing both things at once? Couldn't he be speaking one thing to the disciples and another thing to the gathered crowd?" I would like to think Jesus was gifted enough to accomplish that. To assume otherwise is actually to diminish one's view of the kind of teacher Jesus was. Is it even conceivable that he could tell such a terrific parable that so deftly reveals one's own response to the gospel, and actually not have intended for it to do that? That pushes credulity. Isn't the whole idea of a parable to create a space of disconnect and connection at the same time? To be speaking at multiple levels? I would think that is true of effective speaking and teaching in general, and of Jesus' approach in particular.

The dogmatic approach of seeing every single text of the Bible as having one—and only one—possible interpretation was a bit heavy-handed for me, not to mention a bit daunting, as one had to constantly worry whether or not one had it right. I pushed back a bit in class, but looking back, perhaps not hard enough. If I were sitting in that class today, on the hot seat, having just preached a sermon for the first time, I might say, "Isn't it a bit presumptuous to say that a text has only one possible interpretation, and that you know it? Isn't it a bit incredible to think that writers from thousands of years ago in a different language and culture had one thing on their mind and you know what it is?" I might mention that the rabbinic interpreters of old said that the text has seventy faces. The idea being that Scripture is endlessly deep, with many nuances and levels of meaning, and that you can approach the same text many, many times and it may well say something different each time. I should have asked him—had I not been intimidated by my first year student status and his tenured and nearly retired professor status—"Doesn't the very idea of a parable defy common interpretation and classification?"

What I know now, and perhaps grasped intuitively then, is that a parable is an art form—not a scientific treatise with one, and only one, measurable thesis. It is a dance, a display of shadow and light, a subversive form of speech meant to speak at various levels and elude simple graspings and defy conventional wisdom. I've heard Jesus' parables referred to as "first-century minimalist art." Short. Powerful. Provocative. And just as in any art, it will have shade, nuance, and complexity. It will reveal different things upon different viewings; if you stand in a certain place it may say something different. In the end, it is anything but simple.

Am I overstating the case here? Probably. I'm sure this professor was well aware of much of what I've said here, as he'd been studying the Bible far longer than an upstart like myself. He advanced a very good interpretation of the above parable in question. It may well be the best way to understand it. But is it the only one? And does he know it for sure? OK, just had to get that off my chest. I assume I won't be invited to teach a preaching class any time soon, so there you have it.

THEOLOGICAL BLINDERS

I recall mentioning to someone once that I was studying some Jewish rabbinical writings and commentary on the Torah, and the response was, "Why would you do that? What do they know? They didn't follow Jesus, so obviously they can't have anything to offer us. Why don't you study Calvin's commentary on the Pentateuch instead?"

This air of superiority permeated the environment I grew up in. It is rooted in something that seems to happen frequently in varied branches of Christianity—a sense of theological (and ideological) supremacy. We believe what we believe is true, i.e., Christianity, and that we happen to believe the most true version of it. This attitude seems to create a sort of inbred theological mentality, where we only study people who are writing in our particular tradition.

Why study Jewish commentary and rabbinical writings on the Torah? Because it is a Jewish book! The answer couldn't be more obvious. Yet our theological blinders prevent us from seeing the obvious, and we stunt our own spiritual growth by depriving ourselves of such precious insights and resources.

One small example is studying the background to the Pentecost event in the New Testament. Growing up, I only ever imagined this event as a Christian occurrence that began some days after the death and resurrection of Jesus. Pentecost was a Christian historical occurrence. Once I had to preach on Pentecost (despite my occasional complaints about preaching, getting to study the text and share insights about it is a real blessing—one of my favorite things). I began to find out that in fact Pentecost was an ancient Jewish agricultural festival, known as Shavu'ot.

Shavu'ot means "weeks" in Hebrew, and it was named that because it was a festival that happened 7 weeks after the Jewish feast of Passover. It is a rich event (still celebrated by Jews today) with theological depth, historical connections to the giving of the Law on Mount Sinai (that primal, formative event in Jewish history), and it had earthy, agricultural connections as well. I never knew that there was a Jewish tradition noting that when God gave Moses the Ten Commandments, tongues of fire went out representing the languages of the world. I had somehow overlooked the appearance of wind and fire at Mount Sinai in Exodus 20, which is so clearly connected to the Pentecost experience in Acts 2. That tells me a ton about what the author of the book of Acts is saying about this event in the New Testament, and shows that the second half of the Bible is intimately connected with the first. What other connections in my own Scriptures have I missed because of my unwillingness to engage other traditions?

OUTSIDE PERSPECTIVES

Paulo Freire has noted that when we open ourselves up to outside perspectives, we undergo a "conscientization," or epistemological shift, that moves us from *doxa* to *logos*, or from "opinion" to "knowledge," which allows us to demythologize the assumptions that underlie our perspective, which may or may not be worth continuing to hold on to. This critical reflection is absolutely necessary, says Freire, if we are to move from passive victims of history to truly historical subjects, agents of humanization in a dehumanizing society. In this way, conscientization turns into praxis, as we "reflect and act upon the world in order to transform it."[3] In other words, fresh and different perspectives about God, about the Bible, about anything can take us to new and important places. Pub Theology is a forum for exactly that.

A big part of what Jesus was inviting his followers to join, it seems to me, was the present unfolding of the kingdom of God. He often used subversive stories to do so. The parable of the Laborers in the Vineyard is often read as an allegory. The owner of the vineyard who gives the same wages to those who worked all day as to those who came last is generally understood in the same way. The owner represents the gracious God who gives the same grace to people who convert at the end of their lives as to those who believed early on. Or that the Gentiles who come into the kingdom late are as privileged before God as the Jews, who were God's people from the start. The story speaks powerfully at this level.

Yet this reading fails to take into account the socio-political and economic situation. Jesus is speaking to poor peasants, by and large. Many of these listeners have been displaced from their land through the economic policies of the Roman Empire in the first century. The owner of the vineyard would have been seen as the source of injustice to this audience of peasants and displaced farmers and day laborers. With this background, a question has to be asked: who would they have sided with in hearing this story? Would it not be with those who were dealt the injustice? With those whose voices are silenced, told to "take their pay and go" and are shamed by the landowner? It had happened to them all too many times.

So perhaps this and others of Jesus' stories are about what they are actually talking about (we often want to make them earthly stories with heavenly meanings—likely because that makes them easier to digest). In this case, it seems the story is highlighting the injustices perpetrated when those in power hold it over the powerless and even shame them. The story ends with the owner asking "Am I not allowed to do what I choose with what belongs to me?" If the owner is speaking to former free peasants who have been forced into working as day laborers, his claim to

---

3. Cited in Herzog, *Parables as Subversive Speech*, 22.

the land is "akin to rubbing salt in their wounds," notes William Herzog in *Parables as Subversive Speech*.[4] "How has he gained what belongs to him?" asks Herzog.[5] It seems by playing his role in the systemic oppression of the poor as was increasingly typical in the first century. He may even be forcing them to work land they formerly owned—so these words are a bitter reminder and a slap in the face. Yet by uncovering the source of injustice and telling a surprising story where the workers interact first-hand with one of the often absent, elite landlords, Jesus is empowering his listeners to envision another way.

Similarly, sitting at the table with people who can provide insights from outside our own tradition can allow us to see things from where they are. When we show up with a pile of books—even the Good Book!—full of answers and certainty and arrogance, we turn away anyone from caring about what we have to say, while also missing a unique opportunity to learn from someone who sees the world very differently than we do. Thinking critically about our own assumptions—including about the Bible—is always a healthy thing, and it may just be a kingdom-minded activity.

4. Herzog, *Parables as Subversive Speech*, 93.
5. Ibid.

9

No Doubt

Doubt comes in the window
when inquiry is denied at the door.

— Benjamin Jowett

Doubt isn't the opposite of faith;
it is an element of faith.

— Paul Tillich

We should stake our whole existence
on our willingness to explore and experience.

— Martin Buber

INDOCTRINATION

Growing up in my particular denomination, I was aware of the cerebral nature of our faith tradition from an early age. Cerebral in the
sense that it focused on using our heads more than our hearts, though

61

looking back, it seems our brains were mostly used for storing information rather than thinking. Whether it was memorizing questions and answers from the Heidelberg Catechism, or being able to answer doctrinal questions before the council when I was preparing to make a profession of faith—these things are what constituted the heart of the Christian faith, as I understood it for a long time.

In our circles, what mattered most to parents concerning their children was that (1) we stayed out of trouble; and (2) we memorized the catechism. As long as those two things were happening, it was assumed we were good Christian (Reformed) kids. As far as I can recall, very little was talked about in terms of an actual faith experience. Ours was not a tradition where "sharing one's testimony" was a regularity. In fact, were someone to do so, we all found it a bit embarrassing. Rather than share something personal, we were expected to share a piece of doctrine or a line from John Calvin. Our creeds and confessions and formalized answers seemed to protect us from anything that could be termed an actual encounter with the divine.

Today it seems that two (among many) of the various struggles that churches and faith communities have, regardless of denomination, are: first, how to reach young people, and, second, how to maintain one's particular doctrinal and denominational identity in a world that is increasingly pluralistic and post-denominational, and decreasingly concerned about theological particularities. This latter concern might be a reason that some traditions would be skeptical of a gathering of the Pub Theology sort. Opening people up to other traditions, even within one's religion, could be a threat. What if other traditions prove more attractive? What if people begin to question how and why we've always done it?

But today it is less and less possible to maintain the bubbles that many of these traditions started in. People were limited by geography, knowledge, illiteracy, and poor communication technology. Today those limitations are decreasingly present. And what are these traditions there for? I think at a basic level it is this: to help us know God, know ourselves, know our world, and know our place in it.

But those basic goals often get lost in a tradition or organization's desire to perpetuate itself for its own sake. Sadly, higher goals, such as those just mentioned, get lost in the shuffle. Knowing God takes second place to perpetuating the life of the institution. Ideally these things would not be at odds, but too often they are.

Something that Pub Theology has done for many of us is help us separate out what is simply tradition for tradition's sake, and what seems to be of genuine use in one's spiritual and personal development. Questions such as "What does it mean to know God?" when asked in an open environment, go a long way toward helping clarify some of these issues. Is knowing God the equivalent of knowing the creeds and catechism? Is it being deeply aware of the historical and theological distinctions of a particular faith tradition? The more I mused on these things in my own life, the more I began to wonder whether an overemphasis on knowledge of this sort could be a hindrance to this goal of knowing God, rather than, as we were told, the very means.

Personally, it was not in catechism class that I first really encountered God. It wasn't in brooding over the theological nuances and complexities of predestination or election. It wasn't in focusing on "what my only comfort" was in life and death (the first and most beloved question of the Heidelberg Catechism on which I was raised)— because honestly, memorizing all of these Q & A's was of very little comfort, partially due to my perfectionist nature and wanting to always get it exactly right. None of that penetrated my heart. None of that impacted my soul. It was all just a lot of "right answers." But what good are answers to questions you've never asked? What good are a list of theological definitions of God when you've never actually encountered him? Faith was something I could define and give a nice, tight theological formulation of, but did I actually have it? There was a sense in which I knew a lot about God, but didn't actually know him. It seems to me that my church experience was geared to achieve exactly that.

It wasn't until I was out from under this rigid system that I was in a position to have an actual spiritual encounter. It wasn't until I had encountered other ways of seeing and knowing God among friends of various theological backgrounds that it occurred to me that something was seriously lacking in my so-called faith life. It wasn't until I gave up worrying how much I knew about God that God seemed able to penetrate my life. Once I was able to open my mind to other ways of seeing and experiencing God, things begin to happen. Once I faced the very real fact that faith was something that you live, not something you define, only then did my spiritual life begin to have real traction. Only then did it seem that I really encountered God. And in that moment, it really didn't matter how you defined it, or what they said about such encounters back in the late Middle Ages in Germany, or during church councils in the Byzantine era. This was real. This was now.

It seems to me that this kind of encounter was what captured the hearts and minds of the early disciples, and of the early Christians in Jerusalem, Galilee, and various parts of the Roman Empire. Knowing God had nothing to do with answering a bunch of questions about God. It had to do with a transformative encounter. A relationship. How you de-fined that was of little consequence. (Though sadly it didn't take long for endless definitions to take precedence.) The life, death, and resurrection of Jesus was a point of divine convergence with our world. The ongoing impact and relationship with the man from Galilee was what fueled the movement.

For many of these earliest Christians, it didn't matter whether Jesus was defined as fully God, fully man, or as co-equal with the Father, or whether this remarkable life was the embodiment of the second person of an as-yet-to-be articulated Trinity. These thoughts were not even on the radar, and when they did show up, there was remarkable divergence on the topic. Defining exactly who Jesus was, let alone deciding whether or not God had chosen from all eternity who was to be lucky enough to be part of the in-crowd (conveniently often those making this theological doctrine) was not the main concern. If you had asked any of those ques-tions in the late first century to a collection of disciples, they likely would have responded with quizzical looks on their faces, shrugged their shoul-ders, and gone about the business of living and declaring the kingdom.[1]

So what does it mean to "know" God? It helps to consider the differ-ence between knowing an object and knowing a subject. Peter Rollins, in *How (Not) to Speak of God*, notes, "during the Second World War, prison-ers in concentration camps were treated by the guards as mere objects. These guards possessed a vast amount of data concerning such things as their prisoners' age, previous occupation, family background and siblings."[2] But what kind of knowing was this? Could such data translate into relationship or even understanding? He continues: "Yet this type of knowledge, however comprehensive, is poverty-stricken when compared to the type of knowledge that the prisoners' loved ones would have pos-

---

1. This is not to suggest that they didn't have issues of concern, such as, "Is this strictly a Jewish movement? If not, how do we incorporate outsiders?" And so on. They did. But their concerns tended to be more pragmatic than esoteric.

2. Rollins, *How (Not) to Speak of God*, 23.

sessed. While some of the guards may have held more objective data about an individual than that individual's own family, the family would still possess a knowledge of the individual which the soldiers could *never* gain, a knowledge that is only opened up in love."[3] (Emphasis mine.)

You're beginning to see, I think, what he's getting at here. Relationships are not about information. Yet how often haven't we approached God in this very way—as if the sheer raw data of theological formulations gathered through the ages will translate into something that transforms. Rollins concludes with this: "God can never be and ought never to be reduced to a mere object for consideration, for in faith God is experienced as the ultimate subject. God is not a theoretical problem to somehow resolve but rather a mystery to be participated in. This perspective is evidenced in the Bible itself when we note that the term 'knowing' in the Hebrew tradition (in contrast to the Greek tradition) is about engaging in an intimate encounter rather than describing some objective fact: religious truth is thus that which transforms reality rather than that which describes it."[4]

"Knowing" for the early believers (in their Hebraic context), meant personal knowledge. It meant that they were in a relationship rooted in an ongoing transformational encounter. It could be summed up in one word: love. That is how 1 John 4:8 can say, "Whoever does not love does not know God." This kind of knowledge is not the same as other kinds of knowing. A physicist can be a terrible neighbor and spouse, yet be a brilliant physicist and have a terrific knowledge of the world of science. His moral life, his living, his actions do not impact his knowledge. Yet knowledge of God is always transformational: "Everyone who loves has been born of God and knows God."[5] This kind of approach is not concerned primarily with defining God, because it rather seeks a life that God is defining.

Our theological articulations are rooted in an ancient desire to name God or the divine. This ancient desire was strong because it was held that if you knew someone's name, you had power over them.[6] This can be seen in the story of Moses at the burning bush and the encounter Jacob has at

3. Ibid.

4. Ibid.

5. 1 John 4:7

6. Rollins, *The Fidelity of Betrayal*, 73.

the Jabbok river. All of our theological formulations represent—at some level—our incomplete attempts at naming God. Might they be rooted, consciously or not, in a desire to control him? If our theological musings were actually able to contain God, then we would no longer be talking about the biblical God, for he is beyond containment. He is beyond definition. He is not that which we can control. As Augustine said in the *Confessions*, "Since it is God we are speaking of, you do not understand it. If you could understand it, it would not be God."[7]

And so I wonder if our continued emphasis on doctrine, or confessional statements or creeds, might ironically be the very thing that prevents us from encountering God in the first place. Much like an oft-repeated prayer can be muttered in one's sleep, rather than leading us to an engaging conversation with God himself (though such prayers are needed and wonderful), so might our theological presumptions keep us from having to "know" God in the biblical sense. Because knowledge of God will always fall short. Take the example of a baby. Rollins notes the situation of an infant who knows her mother, and loves her, and is known by her, yet has no way to articulate that knowing, other than to be grasped and known by her. He rightly concludes, "It is ridiculous to imply that a baby can really only love her mother if she understands her."[8]

It is God who knows us, and in being known, we know (in part). There is a world of difference between our understanding of God, and God as He really is. And it is precisely in our continued pride over theological correctness that we find ourselves in opposition to other Christians—let alone adherents of other faiths!—and disconnecting from young people and a culture that couldn't care less about theological precision but care an awful lot about questions of identity and purpose, and the economic, political and social realities of our world, and what faith might have to do with those things.

To clarify, I am not encouraging ignorance—or rejection—of our theological traditions. There is incredible knowledge and wisdom that has come from genuine spiritual experience over the ages. Ancient spiritual practices and ideas remain some of the best we have. We ignore them to our own peril. My concern is more with established theological formulations and certainties than with sage wisdom and practices.

7. Wills, *Saint Augustine*, 9.
8. Rollins, *How (Not) to Speak of God*, 18.

So what I am saying is this: if we could get over our preoccupation with theological knowledge and correctness, perhaps we would find ourselves being engaged by the source of all of our speculation. And as he (or she) engages us, we may well become the articulation of who God is to the world around us. That, it seems to me, is a goal worth pursuing.

EXPLORATION

My experience is not unique. I have had conversations with many people from a variety of traditions who have had similar experiences. And for many of them, the lack of space for asking questions, for divergent thinking, was what led them out of the church—or perhaps out of their faith altogether. What if there was a space where such questioning was not only allowed, but was encouraged?

Many have found Pub Theology to be that very (needed) space. "My own faith, when it is given space to ask, seek, and question comes to life," notes one regular attendee. "When it is forced to concede, comply, and conform, it begins to suffocate." This seems to be a growing sentiment for many. An atheist friend has even noted, "If there were forums like this when I was questioning my faith, I might still be a Christian at some level." For a fellow local pastor, Pub Theology has been a respite amid the expectations of certainty that is put upon clergy. "Here I'm able to be honest about my own doubts and questions, without any backlash. This is the highlight of my week."

What if we approached faith as something not to be gained through indoctrination, but through exploration? For many, this idea sounds blasphemous and provokes fear. Who is guiding the journey? How do you know where you'll end up? What if you believe the wrong thing or land in the wrong place? I wonder if this fear itself doesn't betray a principal understanding of God that those expressing such fear hold themselves—that God is the ultimate source of life in our world, that he is the truth toward which any honest spiritual seeking must lead us, and, that he is sovereign and able to lead us to himself if he so pleases.

Many people have been led to approach God principally by fear. They're told that God relates himself to everyone, but how that all works and where it happens best should probably be left to the experts. To conceive of another way is downright terrifying. You might as well ask them to lead their own expedition to the summit of Everest with no training, no guide, and no equipment. But others realize that God has equipped each of us with the ability to traverse the difficult terrain of life, and enjoy the freedom that comes with searching, learning, and discovery.

Perhaps we need to rethink our understanding of the role of pastors, leaders, teachers, and spiritual mentors. Author Philip Gulley notes, "For too long, the pastor's function has been that of propagandist, perpetuating a party-line view of God that is not always helpful or sound. When the pastor is the mouthpiece for a settled view of God and rewarded for his or her adherence to that view, the incentive to expand our understanding of God is lost, the church becomes spiritually stagnant, and the cause of truth is not well served."[9] Being a pastor, I wince a bit when I read that, because I know how true it is in many cases, maybe at times even with me. Gulley asks us to consider a different view:

> What if we were to think of pastors more as spiritual guides—men and women who help facilitate a community's spiritual journey? This removes the misplaced authority that this role has held traditionally, while still acknowledging that there is a place for having an educated clergy, a theologically robust, intellectually able leader or leaders within the community. Yet this person doesn't become the "expert" who always has the answer, but rather one who has access to the resources to point people in the proper direction as they develop their own spiritual growth.[10]

In contrast to simply thinking of faith as a list of answers in which one doesn't have to think for himself, "healthy religion, and its leaders and teachers, should equip us to move beyond our stunted views of God so we are better suited for life and living."[11] I wonder further whether such a setting as Pub Theology might allow us to realize that there are spiritual leaders and guides all around us—that a neighbor, a co-worker, a friend, and not just one's pastor—might have something to teach us about God. The objections pop up: "But they're not educated. They don't have the training and the background. They haven't been vetted by the 'system.'" This is true. And I do think there is a place for an educated clergy (or I wouldn't have a job!). We need those who have the training in theology, church history, original languages of the Scriptures, not to mention those

9. Gulley, *The Evolution of Faith*, 33.
10. Ibid.
11. Ibid.

with expertise in counseling, spiritual facilitation, and worship leading. But in truth, the authority placed in such a figure has eroded, and perhaps that is for the better, as such authority has been either misused, or become an excuse for someone not to have to take the journey of faith for themselves. And such a worry—that others can't teach us adequately of God—is rooted in fear.

So let's talk about fear. What happens when fear is a primary ingredient in someone's relationship with God? Often, he or she is constantly worried about doing the wrong thing, about offending God's holiness, or believing the wrong thing, and thus facing God's condemnation and wrath. Gulley notes that an unintended consequence for such a fear-filled approach is often anger, "especially in those people whose view of God is trapped in the amber of childhood. Their beliefs hold up until they encounter difficulties that call into question what they've been taught."[12]

Such persons have been taught that God answers prayers, and that God wants our best, and that God promises to protect us. But then a tragedy or disaster strikes and they or someone near and dear to them is not spared, despite the "childhood assurances of God's active and specific care." When this happens, "they are discouraged from questioning God, are reminded of God's power and wisdom . . . and finally urged to pray even more."[13] The response to all of this can be anger and eventual resentment toward God, who, it seems, didn't come through as one had been led to believe.

Gulley states, "If one's relationship with God is primarily about indoctrination, fear and anger are bound to follow, and 'getting it right' becomes vitally important." This was the experience of faith in which I was raised. The more I've been surrounded by a diversity of spiritual traditions and experiences—of which Pub Theology has played a key role—the more I've realized that "getting it right" is not the whole picture. The more I've begun to think there has to be another way. And as I've looked around, I've discovered that others have tuned into this as well, many long before me. Many of us are wondering what it might look like if one's spiritual journey were guided by a sense of exploration, of discovery, of adventure, rather than by fear, anger, guilt, and the status quo.

12. Ibid., 35.
13. Ibid..

What if 'rightness' were of secondary importance and what was paramount was the freedom to investigate uncharted spiritual ground? What if God were not honored by our commitment to orthodoxy, but by our willingness to traverse the difficult terrain of wisdom and discernment? If that were the case, God would not be owed our fear and submission, but our most probing questions. *True blasphemy would be ignoring our responsibility to engage the world and reality at the deepest level of which we are capable.* It would be to meet creation with apathy, with no appetite for inquiry, knowledge, or enlightenment.[14]

My perception is that in my own tradition we've approached the spiritual life from the opposite direction. Rather than opening ourselves up to new spiritual paths and possibilities, we've said up front that there is no exploring to be done. Why keep inquiring when we already have our "only comfort in life and in death?" This comfort is very meaningful and satisfying for many. Yet it can seem—as it did in my case—to present an approach to spiritual living that is more concerned with making sure everyone has his or her seat belts on rather than whether or not the car is going anywhere. (Safety first!) Meanwhile, those who are genuinely seeking, those who are brave enough to leave the parking lot, are seen as "lost" and in need of "saving." Somewhat ironic.

BLOWS WHERE IT WILL

A concern about an approach like Pub Theology, which opens one up to the perspectives of the broader community, is that it may lead to places outside the bounds of traditional orthodoxy. This is a legitimate concern. If we are to rely not just on the educated clergy or the doctrinal councils of long ago, where will we land? What about established, tried and true doctrines? Don't we need an operating baseline understanding if we are going to have a coherent (and cohesive) theological community? There is much to commend this, and given the myriad configurations of every major religion, particularly Christianity, you wonder whether unity is very high on that list of theological priorities.

Let's pick one theological doctrine and examine it. The Holy Spirit. What is it? Is it God? Is it a part of God? Is it another God? Is it the third person of a singular Trinity? Is it something internal to everyone? Is it only in certain people who believe certain things? Is it something like

14. Ibid., 35–36.

intuition? Was the Holy Spirit around in the Hebrew Scriptures, i.e., the Old Testament? Did it come on the scene only after Jesus had left? At the least, it seemed to represent an ongoing, intimate experience of God that the disciples of Jesus and early church community continued to have after his death and resurrection.

An important question is: does this Spirit continue to interact with people today? Many people think so, and I would agree. Yet the ambiguity such a Presence causes cannot be ignored:

> Today any experience of the Divine Presence is ascribed to the Spirit, the third person of the Trinity, whose role, and I'm being only slightly facetious, apparently has something to do with one's denominational affiliation. For instance, the same Holy Spirit who routinely inspires a Pentecostal to speak in tongues hardly ever seems to motivate an Episcopalian to do the same. That same Spirit apparently equips only males to serve as clergy in the Roman Catholic tradition, while routinely calling Methodist women to pastoral ministry. It is an odd and capricious Spirit, indeed.[15]

The issue here is not with the Spirit, which many of us have experienced, but with the church's varied—and often confusing— attempts to define the presence of God in the doctrine of the Trinity. The truth is that not one single person has a corner on who or what God is, and even the biblical writers articulate differing pictures of what encountering the presence of God is actually like. It seems that the church, in seeking to control people's religious experience, "has qualified it, attempting to corral in cold, precise language a presence that 'blows where it will.'"[16] Indeed. It seems that every time we try to limit God, he exceeds all such limitations.

The difference between an indoctrination approach to faith (where the focus is on getting it right) and an exploration approach to faith (where the goal is to experience God in a way that is life-affirming, gracious, and for the good of those around us) seems obvious, once you've experienced it. Pub Theology has been a crucial component in this development of my own understanding of faith. The diversity of spiritual traditions have opened up new paths, the questions I'd never thought to ask (because in my mind they'd been answered) have helped me reconsider some things I thought I had figured out. All of this has created a hunger in me to realize

15. Ibid., 80.
16. Ibid., 81.

that God is bigger and beyond the lines that I had drawn. This realization has rekindled and nourished my faith in important ways.

It is amazing to me that something as simple as beer and conversation could have such meaningful consequences on the pursuit of faith. A faith that open us up to a divine reality—and a broader human connection—that can be missed in our insistence on dogmatic indoctrination. No doubt about it.

10

Found and Lost

Reflections on the Spiritual Merits of Losing Your Way

All journeys have secret destinations
of which the traveler is unaware.

—Martin Buber, *The Life of the Hasidim Said*

The world is a book,
and those who do not travel read only a page.

—Saint Augustine

Unless we change the direction we are headed in,
we might end up where we are going.

—Chinese Proverb

I recently traveled to a relatively large city that I was unfamiliar with: Belfast, in Northern Ireland. I had never been there before, so I watched a Rick Steve's video on the region, perused a guidebook or two, and picked up a map of the city at the airport. All the usual things one does when entering unfamiliar terrain.

My first instinct was to chart out a plan for what to see in the city. So I made a list in my head. First stop: a used bookstore near Queen's University, which was a gem of a place—old dusty books, some on shelves, some scattered haphazardly; dirty, marked-up tables with melted candles on them serving as both cafe and reading area. I nearly picked up an old Paul Tillich volume, but it proved to be out of my budget, not to mention a bit hefty to lug around the city, so I settled on a paperback for three pounds—*Violence*, by Slavoj Zizék.

Next I wandered over to the University to sit in on a class. Somehow I ended up in a lecture for Accounting 101 rather than "Irish Culture in Art and Image" (so much for planning!). Fortunately Zizék got me through the class. Then I stopped in at a pub for some food and my first Guinness in Ireland, as recommended by the guidebook. Great stuff. So far so good. All according to plan (mostly).

The next day I decided to do it a little differently. I left the guidebook in the hotel room. I refused to consult the map. I stepped out the door onto the street, and amidst the busyness of taxis, buses, and pedestrians, acted like I knew where I was going. I had no idea. I just walked. And walked. And walked. And as I walked, with no real destination in mind, I began to notice the shops, the pubs, the people. I saw several old churches. City hall. Turned up an alleyway. More shops. Should I keep going this way? I have no idea where I am. Yet as I was getting more and more "lost," I felt a profound excitement —this was new territory, there were places to discover, and I felt as though on the edge of discovery. This was a journey. This was living. Planned is certainly OK, but the unknown somehow allures.

Is this not true in relationships? The relation to the other, says John Caputo, is "bracing but risky business." He gives an example: "When you get married, you are saying 'I do' not only to who this person *is*, or who you think this person is, but to whomever or whatever this person is going to *become*, which is unknown and unforeseen to the both of you."[1] This is true in all relationships, though perhaps especially in my own case. When my wife and I were married we had known each other for less than a year! It would still be two more months until it had been a year since we

---

1. Caputo, *What Would Jesus Deconstruct?*, 45.

met. Even then, it took us three months or so to start dating. There was much to learn about each other that had to happen after we took that leap of faith (and will remain the case for the rest of our journey together). Fortunately, it has worked out very well in our case. But there are never guarantees. Caputo agrees: "It's a risk—what the philosopher Emmanuel Levinas called a 'beautiful risk'—yet a risk all the same. This willingness to go forward despite (and perhaps at some level because of) the risk is what leads us to call it beautiful."[2] If you knew everything was going to work out happily ever after, it'd be a no-brainer. But this is rarely, if ever, the case. Caputo quips, "If it were a sure thing, it would be about as beautiful as a conversation with your stockbroker."[3]

I keep walking. Another street. Another small alley with stone pavers. What's this? A pub/café with outdoor seating. Old wooden tables. Flower beds awaiting spring. A man standing outside, smoking. I thought, "Why not?" and went in. Inside it was much like a traditional pub. I walk up to the bar.

Bartender: "What'll you have, mate?"

"Do you have coffee?"

"Sure, Cappuccino, Latte, Americano."

"I'll have an Americano—for outside."

"Right then."

I ended up having an enjoyable couple hours outside this small cafe, eating lunch, reading Zizék, and drinking good coffee. I thought to myself, "What a great find this place is—I need a photo." I asked the guy standing outside—still smoking—to take my picture. We started to talk. I introduced myself as Bryan, and he said, "I'm Brian as well." After complimenting each other on our great names, he asked why I was there, and I mentioned something about a conference on theology. Said I was a pastor. He said, "I grew up strictly religious, but I'm an atheist myself."

It being a Thursday, I asked him if he had a good question for my friends meeting that night at the pub back in the States. He answered by way of telling me about a book he had written: *A Dream of Jesus in My Cocktail,* or something to that effect (still seeking publication). It's about three missionaries to South Africa who refuse to engage in the physical and social challenges facing the people, but merely offer them the panacea

2. Ibid.

3. Ibid.

of hope after this life. Then the question: "Is it wrong to delude people if the delusion is serving the greater good?" In his mind, the serving up of false religious hope to allow one to cope with one's present sufferings, rather than attempt to actually address them, was not only inappropriate—it was immoral. Yet the church has a history of this kind of behavior, and it so devastated this man that he left his faith behind and wrote a book about it.

After talking awhile, he had to head to work. He worked for the BBC in Northern Ireland. Interestingly, his station would interview me and several others at our theological conference later in the week. He had to go, but I had the afternoon free, so I had another Americano and kept reading. Later the weather began to turn, so I decided to head out and explore a little more. I came across a few other nooks and crannies, and some that came in handy later in the week. I learned the city with my feet rather than from a book. I saw it with my own eyes, not just on TV. I got lost. And in getting lost, something was found. Here I was at a conference which was exploring new ways to articulate the journey of faith, about exploring the sometimes fuzzy edge between theism and atheism, and I run into a local man who grew up religious and thinks he has left all that rubbage behind, yet clearly has not. Here I was across the ocean missing out on my own Pub Theology gathering, while inadvertently talking theology with an Irish atheist at—where else? A pub. A terrific discovery that could never have been planned or even foreseen.

I wonder how this relates to our spiritual journeys. My sense is that traditionally we like to go "by the book." In other words, we're on a journey, but the trail has already been blazed. All we need to do is look for the signposts left by all who have gone before. The discovery is all done. The theological trail has been marked. Just as there are no explorers discovering new continents on our planet anymore, so it seems there is no new spiritual territory to discover. In *What Would Jesus Deconstruct?*, John Caputo asks, "When is faith really faith?" Great question, and I don't have a simple answer for that. His response: "Not when it is looking more and more like we are right, but when the situation is beginning to look impossible, in the darkest night of the soul."[4] In many circles I have been in, we didn't let people come back who admitted to having a "dark night of the

---

4. Ibid., 45.

soul." We needed security. Certainty. Unquestionable Truth. And we had it, or so we thought.

But I wonder what kind of a journey this really is? Caputo ponders the nature of a journey: "If you knew very well where you were going from the start and had the means to get there, it would almost be like getting there before you even set out, or like ending up where you were all along."[5] Indeed. If it's all charted territory, and there is no discovery, is it actually a journey? Or are we willing to traverse places where there are bends in the road around which we cannot yet see? It seems to me that this is the essence of what faith is about. Faith is what led Moses to lead the people through the desert along paths that didn't always go straight. Faith is what led Jacob to wrestle with God before dawn. Faith is what led Abraham to leave family and familiarity behind for the unknown. If the path is already lit, if there are no moments of darkness, if the map has been drawn—then what need would there be for faith? True faith, at its core, involves radical trust. So if there is no element of risk, no venturing into the unknown, then our spiritual journeys have never really left home. Caputo continues: "Going to a place we already know how to reach or going with a tour guide who has mapped out every stop along the way, or along a paved road with guard rails, rest stops, and food stands where everyone speaks English, is hardly a journey at all."[6] I couldn't have said it any better.

This extends not just to our personal faith lives, but to our faith communities as well. My experience in being part of starting a new church is that many people inevitably ask, "So what is the long-range plan?", "What's next?", or "Where is this thing going?" The understood (and hoped-for) answer generally has to do with stability, growth strategy, money, perhaps even a building. My usual answer has been, "I don't know exactly." We know what things we value, what kind of ethos we are seeking to have as a community, but as to how all that plays out, who knows? Indeed, who can know, as we have not yet been there. We seem to want to squeeze out any room for the Spirit, which Jesus noted "blows wherever it will." We eschew the need for actual faith. We want to know if we're investing in something that is "going to make it," or "headed for success," otherwise we'll invest our time and energy elsewhere. So much for risk. So much for

5. Ibid., 52.
6. Ibid., 53.

faith. Caputo puts it this way: "The more credible things are, the less faith is needed, but the more incredible things seem, the more faith is required, the faith that is said to move mountains."[7] Faith is scary, even dangerous, and it is a platform such as Pub Theology that allows some of us to explore the boundaries of the familiar, to edge into that dark and scary territory that is the unknown.

And so as I wandered around Belfast with no real idea where I was going, it felt as though I were really on a journey. What was around the bend? Where would this street lead? Where would be my next stop? Who would I meet? Would I be safe? The times that were not mapped out and were not on the itinerary were some of the highlights of my trip (we'll have to save the story of Pete Rollins getting us lost on the way back to Belfast from the North Coast for another time). It was the moments in which I was, as Caputo might say, "creatively adrift," and on a true adventure, in which the "incoming" of something unforeseeable was made possible. That is a journey worth taking, or as my friends at Ikon—an eclectic faith community in Belfast (that meets, of course, in a pub)—would sing: "I once was found, but now am lost."

7. Ibid., 45.

11

The Power of Posture

The living are soft and supple;
the dead are rigid and stiff.
In life, plants are flexible and tender;
in death, they are brittle and dry.

Stiffness is thus a companion of death;
flexibility a companion of life.
An army that cannot yield
will be defeated.
A tree that cannot bend
will crack in the wind.

The hard and stiff will be broken.
The soft and supple will prevail.

—Tao Te Ching, verse 76

It started innocently enough, as many disagreements do. Or perhaps conflict is a better word. In any case, it was a morning. And that perhaps was the problem. How I ended up with a gig that requires me to be awake and speaking publicly before noon is one of the great mysteries of the universe. Some guys in our community have met regularly for coffee at 7:00 a.m. at a local coffee shop. The conversation one particular morning was surprisingly theological. Somehow the Bible came up. Specifically, the first couple of chapters.

"It's so obvious that God created the world."

"How anyone with a brain can look out the window and believe in evolution is beyond me."

"The Bible clearly states that God created the world in six days, so I don't know why people just don't believe that."

"You can't be a Christian and believe in evolution."

Ahem. That was me clearing my throat. Or almost choking on my blueberry scone.

"I do."

"You do what?"

"Believe in evolution."

Now being the only pastor present at the gathering, I knew this might come as a surprise to some.

"What?!"

"Well, I think it's a bit foreign to the text to imagine that it has anything whatsoever to do with the process of how the universe actually got started. It's a story written by a people who had a particular view of the world, and this story made sense of their way of seeing the world. The concern of the author was not to say, 'Here's how the universe started scientifically.' which wasn't even a category of thought at the time; rather, it was to say, 'Our God is the one who started the universe, not these other gods.' It was a competing narrative over against other creation stories. It was a poetic declaration of *who* started the universe, not a scientific treatise of *how* the universe started."

"Uhhh . . . I think we need to be more faithful to the Bible."

At this point I realized it was perhaps too early in the morning for this conversation. Or that, as we noted earlier, I should have responded with some questions, and sought to really listen and understand before launching into my little lecture. I also realized it was the last time some of these guys might attend our coffee time. The conversation on that topic ended fairly awkwardly, and I stood up and excused myself.

"I, uh, need to go get a refill on my coffee."

In retrospect, I'm fairly certain I could have had a much better way to engage my fellow coffee drinkers on that morning. I'm not sure I persuaded anyone, and I'm quite sure I alienated one or two of them. By now you are aware that this is not so much a book about a particular theology as much as it is about an approach to theology. In other words, how do I hold my theology? How do I maintain my own convictions in the midst of such divergent opinions? Some are threatened by the very ideas put forth here, of dialogue with people of divergent views of on such important matters. Yet engage and dialogue we must.

I have found that, for me, the best way to do this is to use provisional language. "What is provisional language?" some of you are asking. Well, the first sentence in this paragraph is an example. Provisional language is where you couch or preface a statement with a phrase such as, "It seems to me," or "From my perspective it seems . . ." This approach is much softer and more inviting than black and white statements such as I made earlier, or statements like, "God says x or y," or "The Bible says it, I believe it, and that settles it!," as if somehow you alone are privileged to know exactly what the Bible says and what it means when it says it, despite the widespread divergence across the denominational and theological spectrum over centuries of theological discussion and development. Further, you can speak in third person, such as, "Historic Christianity has tended to say . . . ," where you are citing an outside authority rather than yourself, which defuses any sense of presumption on the part of the speaker.

You might say, "Well, listen, I have strong convictions, and I just need to tell them to people!" Very good. Now imagine someone coming to your door stating very strongly that they know exactly which kind of car you *must* drive, or whether you *must not* drive a car at all, lest you destroy the environment and the world around you and continue our total dependence on fossil fuels from developing nations in the Middle East. I imagine they wouldn't get very far into their diatribe before you'd feel completely annoyed and close the door on them, thank you very much. You may actually have had points of agreement with said person, but their imposing and obtrusive approach would block any meaningful interaction.

The issue is not about convictions, and whether or not one should have them or how strongly one should hold them—we all have convictions about all kinds of things! It couldn't be otherwise. I feel very strongly about certain topics, not least of which is my faith. Yet it remains crucial to consider *how* I go about sharing those convictions. If I try to railroad someone in a conversation, she is not going to care what my convictions are, nor suddenly be ready to repent and pray the "sinner's prayer." An open conversation, it seems to me (provisional language!), allows space for the one you are speaking with to comfortably feel otherwise, while at the same time communicating your conviction with sincerity. If someone feels attacked, they are more likely to become defensive and close down—exactly the opposite of what you want if you are trying to convince someone of something, or if you want someone to consider something in a new light.

Now, some will say this is just pussyfooting around and being wimpy with the gospel. After all, didn't Jesus get hot and bothered with people and call them out, even going so far as to call them sons of hell? Yes, there apparently were some such occasions. But Jesus tended to save that kind of language for the people closest to his own position—for people within his own faith tradition who were abusing their position. And perhaps there is a time and place for this with people of your own theological tradition. But here I am more concerned with Jesus' attitude toward strangers, toward outsiders, toward people who were not normally invited into the spiritual spaces and theological conversations of their world. This approach was always marked by openness, by invitation, by hospitality. And an interfaith dialogue, a truly open discussion, works best, it seems to me (again!), when all present are given the space to hold their present convictions, while also being invited to consider others. It's about respect.

When I consider my own spiritual journey, and people who have influenced me the most, it is the ones who were forceful and loud and full of what you might call "obnoxious conviction" that impacted me when I was younger. It was more impressive, and seemed to be so full of force that it just had to be true. However, as I've grown I've learned that loudness is not an indicator of how true or wise one's convictions are, and in many cases increased volume may well be an indication of how tactless or closed-minded the person is. The less you know of the world and of other faith traditions and of various philosophical outlooks, the easier it is to be convinced you are right. The more you learn, the more you open yourself up to hearing from people of various faith traditions, to people who have sworn off faith, to people who have wrestled with the great questions of existence, the more you realize that there must always be a kernel of doubt in your faith. "I believe x and y, but I could be wrong." That is what you learn. (Or at least what I've learned.) You learn that it could well be that we have all got it wrong, and there may actually be some grand reality of which we know nothing, or very little. When someone has read the great philosophers, the various Scriptures of the great religions, when one has walked through a path of serious doubt and questioning and come out the other side with some real but chastened convictions, that is when one begins to learn the epistemic humility required of us all. This simply means having humility when it comes to discussing what we can know and how we can know it.

The person who says, "But I just know that X is the way it is . . ." or "I don't need to explore other things because I already have the truth," or "Everyone can't be right, so obviously I am the one who is right out of everyone," I (and many others), will be inclined to respectfully let them have their say, but will be less than convinced that they actually know what they are talking about. I perfectly agree that everyone can't be right, and I include myself in that category! To do less is dishonest. That doesn't mean I think I'm wrong. Rather, it means I grant that I may well not have the entire corner on the truth, or perhaps even any corner. I trust that I am on the right path, but am open to correction. I trust that my continued pursuit of truth and wisdom will one day lead me to a higher path than the one I currently trod, and I must be open to such truth and wisdom when and where it may arise. One thing Pub Theology has taught me is not to write off anyone as someone from whom I cannot learn.

That said, everyone clearly cannot be right on a given issue, as people believe very different things, some of which contradict each other. But just because not everyone is right does not mean that one particular group is *exactly* right. It is in fact more likely that we all have some valid insights, and are on to something, but in truth we may all be off the mark in small or large ways.

"What about the Bible?" some of you are thinking. "We have that, and that is God's Word, so clearly those of us who affirm the Bible are right." Well, slow down for a moment. We've already discussed this, but let's recap. What is the Bible? A book. Yes, but a strange book, at that. It is—as we've noted—actually many books, or many writings, rather, that are compiled into a book. So it is more like a collection of books that have developed over long periods of time, written by various authors in various languages over various centuries and in various cultures. I believe that it is a book written and edited by and compiled and canonized by people who were seeking after God. But it was written by people. Let us not forget that. Even the staunchest fundamentalist cannot claim that the Bible was not written by people (at least not without losing all credibility). It is not a magical golden tablet written by a divine hand that someone uncovered on a hillside somewhere. We know that. So all claims to the supposed perfection of Scripture must at least grant that people were involved, and we all know people. If anything, as a Christian I have to admit that Muslim claims to having a holy book are at least as strong, if not stronger than my own. The Qur'an allegedly came to one person as dictated by an angel, and one could argue (as many do!) that this is a more plausible claim to divine origin than something like the Bible, with its multiple authors and occasionally competing or divergent readings.

Yet given all those provisoes I do believe that the Bible is from God. Or at least it was written by people as they were inspired by the Spirit's involvement in their lives. I do not think it was dictated, and here is where I get great comfort in the Judeo-Christian Scriptures over and above the Muslim Scriptures. It was written by real people, with real struggles, in real-life situations in which they involved something of themselves. It was written by people I can relate to. Imperfect people, who were vessels of the divine. It was not dictated to one person—which in many ways would require much less faith and much more slavish devotion. The Bible, rather, is a narrative, a story of the interaction of people with their God, a story which one is invited to enter. A book dictated by a divine source to a single person would seem rather harsh and uninviting to me—not to mention much easier to be the figment of one person's imagination—with all due respect to the Qur'an and my Muslim friends.

"But are there things that you can know absolutely?" asked a Christian at a recent gathering at the pub. "Are there absolute truths?"

An atheist responded: "Yes, there are absolute truths, but is anyone able to know them absolutely?"

This is a subtle point, but one that Christians need to take to heart. Too often we barge into conversations about the gospel with the feeling of invincibility and arrogance.

"Duh, of course I have the truth, God revealed it to me."

"Yes, I know the truth, I believe the Bible."

Such statements might go over OK in the church parking lot, but not in real, honest conversation.

Unfortunately, many people of faith have never considered the fact that things may not be this simple. They are told week after week, Sunday after Sunday, to simply "believe." And further, they are told that the content of that belief is clear beyond all disputing, and that anyone who says otherwise is clearly out to ruin your faith. But perhaps it isn't that simple.

Another possibility, as someone said at a gathering recently, is that "when you die, you may stand before Allah, or any other god(s), and he or she will ask you how it was to experience life as a Christian, and ask you what you want to do next." In other words, this could be one of several existences in succession. Or an existence in which you are merely in a very realistic dream state from which you will one day awake. Or you may die and be gone, much the same as the rest of the animal kingdom, of which we humans are one particular species. Why should it be so different for us? What makes us think we are the ones who need to live forever? What is it about us that can't imagine a universe without us? It certainly operated fine for millions and billions of years before we were born, and certainly can do it again. These are legitimate possibilities, ones which Christians or any other person of faith must be willing to concede as possible. I don't like this last scenario. It seems a bit sad and nihilistic to me, and my own biblical faith provides me with hope for now and beyond. Yet despite all that, I cannot simply write off this possibility as obviously wrong.

Consider the recent movie *The Invention of Lying*, which humorously and cleverly makes the assertion that heaven is something we simply cannot live without, whether it is real or not. Some dismissed the film as blasphemy. Yet even the Bible (yes, the Bible!) concedes this as entirely possible. According to Scriptural tradition, the wisest man in all of the Hebrew Scriptures, King Solomon, had exactly the same thought: "As for men, God tests them so that they may see that they are like the animals. Man's fate is like that of the animals; the same fate awaits them both: As one dies, so dies the other. All have the same breath; man has no advantage over the animal. Everything is meaningless. All go to the same place; all come from dust, and to dust return. Who knows if the spirit of man rises upward and if the spirit of the animal goes down into the earth?"[1] Even Solomon, or we should say, the writer of Ecclesiastes, could admit, "Who knows?"[2]

In his book, *Preaching Re-Imagined*, pastor and author Doug Pagitt refers to the power of provisional language. He notes that the gospel can be more clearly communicated when we preface our statements with "It

---

1. Eccl 3:18–21.
2. Most scholars agree it could not have been Solomon.

seems to me that . . ." or "This may indicate that . . ." or the like.[3] And he is referring to our language when we speak in worship gatherings. If it is true in that setting, how much more so when we are in a non-liturgical situation, where there are no agreed-upon assumptions about beliefs and perspectives? At the pub, in the classroom, or on the street, such language is critical. This allows one to speak honestly, but in a way that carries gentleness and humility, as one should when speaking about such matters.

In the end, however, provisional language by itself is not enough. Clear communication can still be disrupted, not by what is said, but by what is unsaid. You have to have the right attitude. An attitude of interest, of respect for the other person. Because the reality is, the manner in which you speak and the body language you reveal will speak louder than the words you are actually using. Our eyes often betray our level of enthusiasm and interest when someone else is speaking. If you merely pretend you are interested in what someone is saying, or are just putting up with it so that you can have your turn to speak, even if you are saying the right things, your body may well betray you. This means that provisional language is not just a clever strategy—it has to be rooted in an inner reality.

If you are not genuinely interested in learning from people about new or different ideas, then it is very likely you will tend to see people as targets to convert rather than as people (made in God's image!) to love. From my perspective as a Christian, we insult God when we insult one another. Seeing people as merely items on our agenda of world domination, rather than as unique individuals with hopes, dreams, and experiences, is exactly that—insulting. Christ calls us to love our neighbors as ourselves, heck, even to love our enemies! At the end of the day, isn't that what matters? If someone knows that you care about her and are genuinely interested in what she has to say, then regardless of how the conversation turns out, you've already accomplished a lot.

3. Pagitt, *Preaching Re-Imagined*, 200.

12

A Communal Pursuit

Each of us is encased in an armour
which we soon, out of familiarity,
cease to notice.
There are only moments which penetrate it
and stir the soul to sensibility.

—Martin Buber

Reality is a web of communal relationships
and we can only know reality by being in community with it.

—Parker Palmer

FROM A CERTAIN ANGLE

One of the chores I enjoy least is cleaning the toilet. It's an unglamor-
ous but necessary part of life, particularly with children who are
still working on their aim. I remember one such lovely day when I was
cleaning the bathroom. Cleaning up the counter tops—putting away
toothpaste and toothbrushes, hairbrushes, various toys that end up on
the bathroom counter, his and hers deodorant sticks, and sundry other

toiletries. I kept avoiding the toilet, but alas, there it was. So I got the toilet bowl cleaner and brush out, and after cleaning the seat and rim, prepared for the cleaning out the inside. This is my least favorite part of my least favorite chore. In fact, once, in my vehemence to get this part of the toilet scrubbed to a shine, I actually broke the brush in two. Someone or something had to pay for my dislike for the activity! The brush lost out. (Or did it win? No more toilet duty!)

This particular time I was wrapping up, glad to have this out of the way for another week (is once a week enough?). Everything looked clean, and I had done my duty. However, as I bent over to put the brush away under the sink, I made the mistake of looking back at the toilet. Shoot. From this angle, it wasn't clean. In fact, there was a stain all around it, just under the rim where the water comes out when you flush. From standing above it, it looked immaculate. But from another angle, I could see what formerly had eluded my vision. I thought I had the whole thing covered, and the facts, as far as I could tell, were that I had done a thorough job and the toilet was clean. But another angle, say the perspective of a shorter person, or a child, revealed to me what my own position was blind to.

As I thought about this later, I wondered how this applied to other areas in my life. Take sports, for example. As far as I am concerned, the Detroit Tigers are the best baseball team in the history of the sport. Maybe they don't have the most wins, or the most World Series titles (they most assuredly do not). But they have incredible tradition, the best jerseys in the sport (the old English "D" is classic), and some of the greatest players to play the game: Ty Cobb, Al Kaline, and presently Justin Verlander, just to name a few. Yet someone from Cincinnati could give me quite an argument as to why his Reds are as good or better. Or an Orioles fan, or, heck, even a Cubs fan. (Let's keep Yankee fans out of the discussion.) The point is, from my perspective—having grown up in the state of Michigan spending nearly every summer evening of my childhood falling asleep listening to Ernie Harwell call the exploits of Kirk Gibson, Alan Trammell, and the boys from Motown—no team compares, or could take the place of my beloved Tigers. Yet viewed from another angle, by another person, the team might not rate nearly so high.

What about faith? We like to think that we know quite a bit, that we can see clearly, that our tradition and Scriptures give us clear insight into who God is, and that we don't have much to learn from those of other traditions, let alone those of other faiths. But what if our particular angle doesn't give us the whole picture? Could it be that someone may have access to a view that helps me see what my position blinds me to?

In his book *Introducing Theologies of Religions*, Paul Knitter uses the imagery of a telescope:

> A simple analogy might make all this clearer and reveal its relevance for our issue of dialogue: we might compare "truth" or "the way things are" to the starry universe around us. There is so much of it, and it is so far away, that with our naked eyes, we really can't see what's there. We have to use a telescope. But by enabling us to see something of the universe, our telescope also prevents us from seeing everything. A telescope, even the mighty ones used by astronomers, can take in only so much. This describes our human situation. We're always looking at the truth through some kind of cultural telescope, the one provided us by our parents, teachers, and broader society. The good news about this situation is that our telescope enables us to see; the bad news is that it prevents us from seeing everything.[1]

So what can we do? Well, the answer is surprisingly simple. We can borrow someone else's telescope. Someone else's telescope may be built differently than my own, may have been aimed at a different angle, and may reach areas of the universe that mine was unable to reach or bring into focus. Knitter notes that "the more telescopes we manage to use, the more our vision and understanding of truth will expand. Thus, we come to the conclusion that felt right to us from the beginning: truth is known through conversation."[2]

This is true on many levels, including how one reads the Bible, as we noted earlier. If we assume we can approach a text in our own language and instantly be in tune with what we are reading, while that may be the case occasionally, it can also be the case that we miss much of what is being said. Wes Howard-Brook notes that "poor peasants in Latin America can connect with Jesus' parables drawn with images of farming far more readily than clean-fingered university professors in the United States or Europe."[3] At the same time, "such non-agrarian 'elites' may have an insight into the text due to their expertise in areas of linguistics, history and

---

1. Knitter, *Introducing Theologies of Religions*, 11.
2. Ibid.
3. Howard-Brooks, *Becoming Children of God*, 3.

culture."[4] In other words, even in reading one text, from one tradition, we need to pursue the truth together.

Could we push this even further, and ask whether we need not just other voices in studying one religion's holy book, but other voices from other traditions and other books? Could it be that I, as a follower of Jesus, have something to learn from the traditions surrounding the Buddha? Could it be that if I were to look through a Zen telescope, or a see the world from an Islamic point of view, that I might discover true things about our world that had not shown up as I peered through my own lens? And not just true things about the world, but even true things about faith, about life, about God?

I think we have to posit that this is a possibility. Perhaps even a good possibility. After all, people of many different faiths, and people of no faith, often are normal, happy human beings "getting their jobs done and raising their families as well as, perhaps better than, we are."[5] They are people of integrity, who live and love and long for the best in our world. If Christianity is the only place in the world to find truth, you'd assume that Christians would be the moral exemplars of the world. That we would be the sole lights shining in the universe. A quick review of church history helps us see through such a hagiographic notion. What if, in fact, God has left traces of himself (or herself) in many places? In many people? In all people? Isn't it at least possible that God is present in the earnest prayer life of a Muslim? In the "salvation" a Hindu finds by seeking Nirvana?

Christianity can no longer naïvely assume it has a corner on God. If God was so intent to speak to humanity through one religion, why are there so many?

As William Cantwell Smith asked about fifty years ago:

> How does one account, theologically, for the fact of humanity's religious diversity? This is really as big an issue, almost, as the question of how one accounts theologically for evil—but Christian theologians have been much more conscious of the fact of evil than that of religious pluralism . . . From now on, any serious intellec-tual statement of the Christian faith must include, if it is to serve its purpose, some sort of doctrine of other religions. We explain

4. Ibid.

5. Knitter, *Introducing Theologies of Religion*, 6.

the fact that the Milky Way is there by the doctrine of creation, but
how do we explain the fact that the Bhagavad Gita is there?[6]

This is a threatening question to many traditions that prefer the simplicity, ease, and comfort that comes with already having the whole map of
the universe in your lap. But what if the reality is that you've only got one
part of the map? That's not to say that your map is incorrect, or that even
the particular, historical claims of your faith—my faith as a Christian—
are not indeed the primary means by which God has revealed himself. As
a Christian I believe this is the case. But I can no longer believe that I have
it all, and that others have nothing. As Edward Schillebeeckx puts it: "The
unshaken certainty that one continues to possess the truth oneself while
others are [completely] mistaken is no longer a possibility."[7] He notes that
to say one's own way is the only possibility for grasping religious truth is
to live in a "time warp."

Some will say this is just caving to a pluralistic culture and seeking
not to offend anyone. Maybe. But perhaps it is more a matter of intellectual honesty, as Cantwell Smith notes above. The biblical story itself
often tells of God working outside of the established religious institutions (temple, church, etc.). This happens through the prophets, through
people like Melchizedek (likely priest of a Jebusite astral deity), Rahab (a
Canaanite), Cyrus (a Persian king), Paul (who quotes Greek poets as a
source of understanding about God), and others. God cannot simply be
boxed in to one tribe or institution, even in the biblical story (we should
not confuse primacy with exclusivity). To assume that one tradition alone
possess the means for pursuing a better world, or even for pursuing God,
might not be completely accurate. It would be easier if one group had it
all—at least for that group. But it also perhaps goes against the picture of
a God who "spoke to our forefathers through the prophets at many times
and in various ways."[8]

Has God limited his revelation to humanity to one particular group
in history, leaving the majority of people who ever lived out of the picture? It is extremely difficult to reconcile a God "who so loved the world"
with such a picture.[9] Now perhaps we are not talking about a God of love,

6. Ibid., 13.

7. Ibid., 7.

8. Heb 1:2.

9. John 3:16

in which case anything is possible. But my own tradition of Christianity posits that love is a central part of God's character, even going so far as to say, "God is love," which such selectivity and exclusivity seem to explicitly contradict.

THE COMMON GOOD

I facilitate a professional networking group in my local community. One of the things I often say when welcoming everyone to the group on a given morning is: "We all know more people together than we do on our own." That's the point of networking. You know someone who just moved to town and needs car and home insurance. Someone else is an insurance agent—but not just one you Googled or looked up in the phone book—a friend. Someone you can trust. So you network, and you connect one friend to another friend. It's called synergy, pooling of resources, networking, and there are many professional groups who similarly take advantage of connecting for the sake of a larger benefit.

I wonder if this is possible when it comes to our spiritual pursuits as well. Our pursuit of God, of truth, of what's best for our world. Some would say, "Well yes, and that is the point of the church." I agree strongly that this happens in faith communities, and is in many ways the reason I am not only a part of one, but help lead one. Yet no such community exists in a vacuum. They operate within a context of a specific town or city, many within a denomination or at least theological heritage, and most are comprised of people who originally were in *another* such community, and bring with them all of those experiences and perspectives. All of these things add to and influence each individual community. It is not only possible that those outside of my church impact my faith journey, it is unavoidable. And this is a good thing! Religious communities that cut themselves off from everyone else are generally dismissed as cults. So yes, it is good that one can learn from a neighbor who is a Methodist, or a co-worker who is a Catholic, or even someone from within one's tradition who grew up in Eastern Canada rather than the U.S. Midwest.

But let's go a step further. What about someone outside of one's faith tradition? Could a Muslim, a Buddhist, or an atheist actually help me to see the world better, to get closer to God, and to seek the common good? Brian McLaren notes that a generous orthodoxy (in his book of the same name), "while never pitching its tent in the valley of relativism, nevertheless seeks to see members of other religions and non-religions not as enemies but as beloved neighbors, and whenever possible, as dialogue partners and even collaborators."[10] In other words, not only ought we to learn from those who are quite different from us, religiously speaking, but we ought not let those differences get in the way of positive interaction, dialogue, and even working together in our communities. The local interfaith group I mentioned earlier, the Area Council On Religious Diversity, has come together to speak out for equality, specifically for a local ordinance which outlawed discrimination based on sexual orientation. This same group is now discussing the possibility of gathering to serve meals to the local homeless population. A Wiccan and a Humanist, a Quaker and a Jew, and many others—all working together for the common good.

WHAT OUR WORLD NEEDS

Occasionally there are events that get everyone talking. Yet where does one go to discuss one's feelings about such events? Sadly, too often we forgo any meaningful conversation about such important topics, and let the people on the television process these events for us. When Osama bin Laden was killed, there were many images of Americans celebrating on the news. Not everyone was comfortable with this. The local newspaper called me to see how our faith community was responding. I noted that we were going to have a conversation about it at the pub that night. They sent a person down and did a story on how locals were dealing with this. We had a good conversation, and our conversation at the pub became a part of the larger community conversation when it was part of an article featuring local reaction on the issue. Having a place to go to talk about important issues is necessary. When such gatherings do take place—perhaps especially within churches and faith communities—the result is often a one-sided discussion, or controversial topics are avoided altogether. "One of the main reasons I was attracted to Pub Theology," notes one regular, "is that it was a group of people willing to talk about serious issues in an informed and engaging way. It is too rare to find people of my own age group who are interested in things other than sports, movies, and video games."

10. McLaren, *A Generous Orthodoxy*, 35.

In addition to global and national issues, there are always important local issues to address. We have had important conversations on things like the above-mentioned proposal that affirms non-discrimination in our city, particularly making it illegal to discriminate based on perceived or actual sexual orientation. Pub Theology became a place to have a meaningful dialogue that undercut the rhetoric involved in what was a volatile subject in our community.

Another instance was a local tragedy in which a teenage girl was killed by a classmate. We needed a place to gather, to grieve, and to talk about how to respond. As we did so, broader theological topics such as what evil is, where it comes from, and how to deal with it became inevitable, perhaps necessary corollaries. Those who came that evening found it to be a very helpful night, and it was a part of helping us grapple with the difficult and sometimes ugly realities we encounter in life.

Pub Theology can be a place to defuse tension, uncover ignorance, and undo stereotypes. In 2011 there was a group claiming to know the exact date of Jesus' return. The so-called rapture. This presented an opportunity for Christians in the group to discuss various perspectives on the "end-times," including sharing the historical perspective that the rapture was a nineteenth century Western evangelical invention which is not supported by the New Testament.[11] Such a discussion makes it harder to dismiss a whole faith tradition because of the extremism of a few. It also helped us realize there were local churches who were vocalizing perspectives that were not that different from these fringe groups, including one prominent church whose pastor encouraged his congregation to "sell everything they had and go on vacation," because Jesus was coming back "very, very soon." Such preaching takes advantage of people and leaves them in a potentially harmful situation, even encouraging the liquidation of homes, property, and other capital which can then conveniently be given to the church, to do with as it sees fit, "just in case" Jesus doesn't come back soon after all.

Another outlandish claim made from the pulpit at a local church was that the 2008 financial collapse was God's punishment on George Bush for conceding that we need a two-state solution between Palestine and Israel. Such religious rhetoric is harmful, unfounded, and needs to be exposed. Often we are unaware that it is happening right in our

11. See N. T. Wright, *Surprised by Hope: Rethinking Heaven, Resurrection, and the Mission of the Church.*

own communities. The best way to counteract such bad theology and uninformed history is by having open conversation which seeks to be historically-rooted, philosophically sound, and connected to the actual tradition it claims to speak for.

In his book *The Church is Flat*, Tony Jones notes that much of the theological impetus behind the emerging church movement is driven by a relational ecclesiology.[12] In other words, people are gravitating toward a communal approach to doing church. Older, authoritative models are increasingly becoming a thing of the past. Part of this is due to "the recent and rapid advent of technological devices (mobile phones, computers, handheld devices) and the 'new media' (websites, blogs, Facebook, Twitter), and the significant generational differences begat by globalization."[13] It is also happening because of the "ready access to theological and biblical resources" which allow people to investigate their own theological questions apart from the auspices of a traditional church hierarchy.

These changes are happening whether we like them or not. Some will bemoan the loss of "how things used to be." They may lament that it is no longer simply a parishioner's duty to show up to a worship service to be taught what to believe, and that attendance is declining at supplementary catechism or other adult education classes, where an expert passes on the nuts and bolts of the tradition. The problem with this approach today is that people are questioning not only this method of passing on the faith to the next generation, but additionally, whether the *content* being passed on in such settings is actually the historic faith, or the faith as one should hold it today, or whether the idea of a historic orthodox faith even exists. Increasingly people are becoming aware of the plurality of expressions present in the roots of their own faith, which may have been presented to them as a monolithic and unified body of doctrines.

One group in particular that might feel threatened by this growing trend of communal approaches to faith might be the clergy. They, after all, are the ones who have had their authority undercut. Yet perhaps fear is the wrong response, notes my friend David, who is a Presbyterian pastor. He notes how Pub Theology can cut through the perceived authority of the clergy: "Pub Theology is helpful to reduce these things that we've taken for granted or maybe we haven't thought through, but they have an

12. Jones, *The Church is Flat*, 1.

13. Ibid.

air of superiority," he notes. "It's good to get rid of those things, because people are searching. I like getting right down to where there actually might be something that I can offer to someone as a fellow traveler on the journey, as opposed to 'I can offer this because I'm a Christian, or I know the Bible, or I'm a pastor,' or whatever."

I agree. Getting to a place where we have something to offer to someone else as a fellow human being who is searching for God, with titles stripped away, might be a good thing. This is not to say titles don't matter or are worthless, as we obviously need experts in various fields, including theology and spirituality. It is to say that we need to acknowledge that much of the implied authority in the past was more than was accorded. I grew up in an environment where the pastor was granted a certain final authority on spiritual matters. Today this is harder and harder to find, as there is a lot of stripping away of that implicit authority. As we talked about this at the pub over a beer, David acknowledged, "I really think that the church has good authority and misused authority. When people say things because they're supposed to, or they hold other people to standards because of something they can't justify very well—well, I think we're at a time where people see right through that." People are owning for themselves what they believe much more than in the past, where it may have just been handed to them. David notes, "And if that's where the culture is going, we have to be able to negotiate that."

My assertion is that this is not just acceding to the culture, of which experts note that the "relation between the individual and the collective is blurred."[14] It is acknowledging that perhaps culturally we are developing a superior approach. One of the things I love about Pub Theology is that it is not limited to what happens around the table on Thursday nights. It bleeds into the broader community, such as the various stories in our local newspaper, a local radio show that featured our group, as well as the conversations that continue the next morning at work or the local coffee shop that were prompted by our communal conversation the night before. Our towns, cities, and world are having a conversation. We would do well to take our place at the table.

A quiet woman, probably approaching retirement age, attended a recent Pub Theology gathering. She said very little throughout the evening, but by the end her eyes were glowing. She noted to a few of us before

14. Jones, *The Church is Flat*, 15.

leaving: "There is a beauty to the coming together of different voices at the table. I feel so welcome here, and sense that others are drawn to this because we need each other. Different voices coming together is what our world needs." I wholeheartedly agree.

13

Slippery Slopes, Sailboats and Safety Nets

A ship in port is safe, but that is not what ships are built for.

—Grace Murray Hopper

DRAWING THE LINE(S)

Our church is part of the Christian Reformed Church in North America. As I've said, this is the church I grew up in, a church with a very robust and distinctly Reformed theological heritage. That being said, our particular community has for the most part embraced the idea of having a faith that is open to scrutiny, with asking the hard questions, with engaging in the kinds of conversations this book has described—in other words, not assuming everything that has been handed to us is never to be questioned or wrestled with. Yet this approach hasn't been without struggles. The question was recently asked: "I appreciate that there is an openness to asking questions in our community, but isn't there a point at which we can point to some definitives and say—these are our beliefs, these are our bottom line doctrinal standards, this is where we draw the line? Can't we have some sort of safety net?" I have heard this question asked by more than one person, and I know that others have had similar concerns.

I appreciate where this question was coming from, and certainly can empathize with the concern. These kinds of questions prompted some great discussion among the leadership of our community. Should we have a doctrinal statement? Should we draw a line in the sand? Should there be a link on our website to "what we believe" or to the doctrinal statements of our denomination?[1]

The discussion encouraged me to write up what we might say if we had such a page on our website. It went like this:

> We have not had an official "statement of faith" at Watershed, for a variety of reasons.
>
> Often "statements of faith" are used as litmus tests to help someone determine whether people are "in" or "out," or whether or not this church "has it right." We tend to believe that statements of faith are often used in this way as a [yard]stick to measure one's orthodoxy, or in worse cases, as a stick to beat people with.
>
> So rather than making a long list of what we do believe or don't believe, we'd prefer to think of a table which gathers us together and invites us in, at which all are welcome, and at which we can experience life together. This table denotes some things that are central to our understanding of faith, but the table is not meant to keep people in or out, but to draw people into the center of life with God. A table evokes things like food, meals, shared experience, laughter, tears, confessions, obsessions, accomplishments, rejections, love and sorrow, bread and wine, newness . . . and community.
>
> On the table, imagine that there are three words written— God, Jesus, resurrection. Those represent what you might call our "working understanding" of the Bible and the life and message of Jesus: that God has presented himself to us through the person of Jesus, who on the cross showed us that God is love, that God is present with us in suffering, and that God sought ultimate justice by submitting to injustice. Yet this could not hold him down, and in the resurrection we find that God is not done with this world, but is in fact, transforming it. All of this can be understood by the declaration "the kingdom of God is at hand," which was central to the message of Jesus.
>
> That is what we come to the table understanding as central to our life as a faith community. The words are somewhat faded, which

---

1. No one has suggested we dismiss our denomination's doctrinal standards or the classic creeds of the church or anything of the sort. The concern was that we had no place on our website that pointed to those or said specifically, "This is what we believe."

denote to us that God is not always obvious in our world, and even how we understand these concepts of God, Jesus, and resurrection are not always cut and dried. There is room for questions, even for doubt, as God is always bigger and beyond our conceptualizations of him, and we all, like Jesus on the cross, experience moments of his absence. We trust that though presently we "see through a glass darkly" one day we shall see "face to face." So while we may each have differing perspectives on various doctrinal issues, our common core understanding is that we encounter God in and through the person of Jesus, that we seek to be disciples who walk in the way of the cross, and that the resurrection means real hope for people here and now and that we can anticipate one day a new heavens and a new earth, a world where God is "all in all."

If that sounds like a life worth living, or a community worth experiencing—we invite you to pull up a chair and join us.[2]

What do you think? Did we pull it off? Is this too open-ended? Or is it too exclusive? The important thing, as far as I am concerned, is that we worked this out together, in community, and came up with something that represented us. It is also important to note what we were not doing. We were not inventing a new creed, a new doctrinal standard, or anything of the like. We would simply defer to the Apostles' Creed and other similar creedal statements if people were interested in those. We were not redefining the *content* of faith, but rather describing the *approach* to faith that our community was taking. An approach that embraces both answers *and* questions.

CHILD-LIKE FAITH

A common reaction to a difficult question about faith is: "Don't worry about it. We just need to 'have a child-like faith.'" The reasoning behind such a response is that there are some questions that we just can't answer, and there's no reason to upset the apple cart by questioning tried and true doctrines and methods that have served us well for centuries. I think there is much to commend in this approach, and agree there will always be an element of mystery when we are talking about God.

Hearing someone make this appeal to child-like faith recently started me thinking back to when I was little. As a child I can recall many special moments. When I entered the living room as a kid on Christmas

2. http://watershedtc.org/whoweare.htm

and found presents under the tree, it was magical. Somehow, some way, Santa came through. It was fun, mysterious, and I was in. What kid isn't?

These moments are wonderful. Perhaps you can remember such a time in your own life. Or if you have kids, as I do, perhaps you know the delight in playing along with the story, vicariously experiencing the joy and innocence once again. My three boys just each handed me a letter to send to Santa with all the things they want for Christmas. I asked them, "Do you think Santa will get these letters?" They nodded in eagerness. In faith. In hope. Even with a bit of child-like trust.

But this belief in Santa can't last forever, can it? I suppose we could all mutually agree to act as if Santa is real. (In some ways, you could say that given our culture's Christmas overkill every year we do exactly that. We reinforce the illusion, by some mutual agreement—which must be some marketer's dream.) It lasts until a ten-year-old who has figured it out says to her younger brother, "You know Santa isn't real, right?" And Christmas is ruined. If only he could go back to his child-like faith.

I wonder if there are parallels to this scenario in the life of faith. Jesus certainly commends children as "the greatest in the kingdom" and calls us to receive the kingdom "like a little child." Interestingly though, the phrase "faith of a child" or "child-like faith" does not actually appear in the Bible, though the idea is certainly present. When taking part in a discussion about hard-to-understand issues or when learning something that might challenge an aspect of one's faith that perhaps had been taken for granted, it can be a comfort to resort to this idea.

"But you just have to have a child-like faith."

OK.

Yes.

But what is a child-like faith?

When Jesus mentions that children are the greatest in the kingdom of heaven, he is noting their humility—not their ability to believe certain things about God, nor their ability to believe almost anything. In Matthew 18 he is contrasting children with those who argue and fight about who is the greatest. (Though I know some kids who have the same argument!)

In Mark 10 he talks about receiving the kingdom like a little child. Here I think the focus is on being open to what God is doing in the world, and that it is those who are powerless, or are willing to lay aside their power, who will receive it. This may be in contrast to those who were skeptical or critical of the things Jesus was doing as he proclaimed the kingdom (teaching, healing, eating with outsiders, etc.), often those who felt secure in their present positions of power. So there definitely is an element of openness and embracing what God is saying and doing, in addition to the critique of power that is so central to the gospels.

We all know there is something about grown-ups that gets in the way of relationships, that makes simple things more complicated, that is less willing to trust, etc. Further, we want something that is easily grasp-able, something that we can hold on to easily, something that soothes and calms our fears.

Even David in the Psalms yearns for the simplicity of a child:

"I do not concern myself with great matters
or things too wonderful for me.
But I have stilled and quieted my soul;
like a weaned child with its mother,
like a weaned child is my soul within me."[3]

There is a time to just sit and rest in God. He is vastly greater than we are, and it is a great comfort to simply trust in his goodness. That is a very biblical thing to do and is one of the supreme joys of faith.

So what are we to do when things get complicated, as they inevitably do? I suppose we could retreat and "find a happy place." Or plug our ears and simply ignore whatever is going on. Or say, "I just want a child-like faith." Or tap our heels and say, "There's no place like home."

But we do not remain children. We grow up.

And that is not necessarily a bad thing.

The Apostle Paul noted as much: "When I was a child, I talked like a child, I thought like a child, I reasoned like a child. When I became a man, I put childish ways behind me."

Some might say faith is becoming "too heady." Perhaps we have Paul to thank for that. Or the church fathers. Or the desert fathers. Or the various councils that met early on to hammer out incredibly heady ideas. Or Duns Scotus. Or Anselm of Canterbury. Or Thomas Aquinas. Or John Calvin. Or the medieval scholastics who wrote volumes and volumes of incredibly dense theology.

The idea that faith is getting more heady is probably not actually correct. In fact, perhaps we are coming out of a time of when the faith has been "dumbed down," and now some are attempting to deconstruct

3. Ps 131:1–2.

a few of the concepts—the rapture, a "personal relationship with Jesus," young-earth creationism—that came out of our dumbing-down period (the explosive growth of fundamentalism in the twentieth century). So maybe there is a reapprehension of the faith taking place. A return to thinking carefully about some things we've simply taken for granted. This might be painful to some, but, in reality this probably happens at some level in every generation.

One might also point out that the very things some call the simple aspects of faith are themselves the results of some very intellectual dialogue, hard work, and intense thinking. Let's take one issue: the Trinity. As Christians we take this aspect of God for granted, but it took *centuries* of thought and argument for this "simple" concept to be worked out. We might take it to be explicitly and obviously biblical, but this may be due in large part to the fact that we are often taught these doctrines before we approach the text. Or consider the divinity of Jesus. Some have noted that similar language used to describe Jesus in the Gospels is used of other figures in Second Temple Jewish literature of the time, without the same implications of full divinity.[4] The doctrine that we take for granted—the Son is of "one substance" with the Father—took centuries to work itself out, and there wasn't always unanimity as it developed.[5] Or pick your favorite "simple" doctrine. The idea that one's beliefs are simple is a nice one, but may well be an illusion. A little exploring reveals that what seems simple (and obvious) to us, is more likely a highly developed theological concept (which does not make it less true or less worth believing, but complex rather than simple).

Even in Jesus' day children were expected to memorize vast portions of the Torah, if not the whole Torah itself. That's way too heady for most of us. And that was the expectation for *children*. So perhaps the faith of a child is the faith of one who takes their faith seriously. Who takes God seriously. Who commits their hearts and minds to knowing God as well as possible, by taking the textual tradition they've been handed seriously, but also, recalling Mark 10, when the kingdom is breaking in around them (even in unexpected ways!)—they are open to it.

We might think that asking hard questions is the opposite of biblical faith. Yet this might overlook the fact that Jesus himself did quite a bit of

---

4. See Thom Stark's upcoming book, *Behold the Man*, Wipf and Stock, forthcoming.

5. The Council of Nicea took place in 325, or nearly 300 years after Jesus' death.

deconstructing of what many took for granted. "You have heard it said . . . but I say to you . . ."

So when we look for cracks in the settled foundations of our assumptions, perhaps we are simply walking in the path of the Jesus himself, who called us to be *as* children, without actually becoming children.

After all, when I was a child, I thought like a child.

But we are no longer children, and we must at some point, put childish ways behind us.

SLIPPERY SLOPES

Often in discussion on matters of faith, when someone hears something that sounds unfamiliar or suspicious, or that challenges a long held belief, they will warn of going down the "slippery slope." Central to this metaphor is the idea that altering one's understanding (or behavior) on one thing, will automatically lead to a very bad situation, where one changes one's beliefs or behaviors entirely. I was discussing this idea with my friend Chris, who is a philosopher. He mentioned, "It's worth noting that 'slippery slope' is the name of a fallacious form of reasoning." I hadn't heard that before. So I asked him to explain.

"The reasoning goes like this. If we do A, then a chain of events will be triggered: B, leading to C, then D, etc., leading to some terrible result Z. Thus, if we do A, Z will inevitably result."

"OK, what's the problem with that line of thinking?"

"Such reasoning is fallacious when *no good reasons* are offered for thinking that each event in the chain really will lead inevitably to the next. Simply fearing that each might lead to the next is not a good reason to think that it will."

"That seems to be what people are often thinking of with respect to questioning religious doctrines."

"Yep."

One example where this often comes up is on how one reads the opening chapters of Genesis. Did God create the world in six literal days? Is the earth actually only a few thousand years old? Some fear that if the literal interpretation of Genesis falls, then other understood interpretations of the rest of the Scriptures would fall like dominos. A more nuanced view of the Bible (as described earlier) would help one see that such a fear is unfounded.

Apparently, unbeknownst to all of us, whether living at or below sea level, or in the Rockies themselves, for that matter, we all dwell upon a mountain. This slippery slope imagery seems to assume we are at the peak, by implying that the only direction we can move is down. But what is the peak? Perfect knowledge and understanding of God? Not even Moses, who did ascend the peak to meet with God himself, had that.

What if this imagery needs to be turned around? What if instead of sliding down such a peak when we discover new ways of apprehending God, we are actually ascending the slope? What if learning new or different approaches to reading Scripture is part of the hike to the top? Could it be that the step being taken is not plunging us headlong into the valley of heresy or doom, but helping us ascend, one small step at a time, toward a closer apprehension of the world and of God? There may be places where the slope is a bit slippery, but even when (and if) this is the case, we have a choice: we could not try to climb at all, or we could choose to climb carefully. For some, the benefits of climbing outweigh the risks. If you're going to climb, though, it's best not to go it alone.[6]

If we are not yet at the peak, isn't it possible that a new understanding is moving us just a bit closer to how things actually are, and hence, toward God? It seems a healthy faith would be one that is constantly seeking, constantly growing, constantly moving. Some prefer the security of base camp to the danger of the cliffs, the comfort of the flat ground to the sheer rock faces that may, from time to time, need to be dealt with. There is nothing at all wrong with that preference—but let's agree to not confuse the base camp with the summit.

SAFETY NET

"But I just need a safety net. I just need to know that there are some bottom line things that never change."

This is a common sentiment—and a good one. I agree that there are bottom line things that never change and are absolutely true about the universe and about God. The philosopher Immanuel Kant describes such absolutely true things as reality-in-itself.[7] Those things are there, or

---

6. I first encountered this idea of turning the slope imagery around at a blog by Justin Topp, in which the idea is anecdotally attributed to Peter Enns. http://musingsonscience. wordpress.com/2010/08/12/slippery-slopes.

7. Westphal, *Whose Community? Which Interpretation?*, 19.

we could hardly have a stable, coherent universe. Only the most skeptical of skeptics would doubt the reality of absolutely real things. Here's the problem: is any one of us able to perfectly apprehend those things? The question is not whether those things are there (they are), but whether or not we have perfect access to them.

Kant differentiates it like this: appearances are the way we see the world. The "thing in itself" is the way God sees the world.[8] Things really are the way the divine mind knows them to be. But not even the most adamant believer would assume that we know as much as God knows. Even the biblical writers were tuned into this: "For as the heavens are higher than the earth, so are my ways higher than your ways, and my thoughts than your thoughts."[9]

It is we who perceive reality through a filter. A filter of categories, experiences, presuppositions, culture, language, and so on. Often we are oblivious to the very things that form the lens through which we see the world, but the lens is there. And over time, our understandings of the world change. (Whether or not God himself changes is a whole other topic—and a great one to discuss over a pint!) It is we who grow, we who learn, we who adapt. Even one's faith today is likely to look a lot different than it did for a fellow believer one hundred years ago, let alone a thousand or two.

Merold Westphal in his terrific book, *Whose Community? Which Interpretation?* notes that "our interpretations are always relative to the presuppositions that we bring with us to the task of interpretation and that we have inherited and internalized from the traditions that have formed us."[10] In other words, none of us start from scratch when we approach a verse in the Bible or a theological doctrine. We see these things through a lens. Westphal notes that "unless we confuse ourselves—as tradition-bearing individuals and communities—with God, we will acknowledge a double relativity: our interpretations are relative to (conditioned by) the presuppositions we bring with us, and those presuppositions, as human, all too human, are themselves relative (penultimate, revisable, even re-placeable) and not absolute."[11]

---

8. Ibid.

9. Isa 55:9.

10. Westphal, *Whose Community? Which Interpretation?*, 14.

11. Ibid.

Some see the word "relative" and immediately confuse this with the idea that "anything goes." This is not the case at all. Simply because our interpretations are affected by historical, cultural and linguistic perspectives, is not to say that suddenly "anything goes," or that one thing is as good as another. It is simply to acknowledge both the limit we have as finite human beings to perfectly grasp the infinite divine, and the fact that we come to believe what we do from within a certain historical, cultural, linguistic context. Westphal says that we must not fall into the place of despair ("anything goes"), nor the place of arrogance (we have "the" interpretation). "We can acknowledge that we see and interpret 'in a glass, darkly' and that we know 'only in part' (1 Cor 13:12), while ever seeking to understand and interpret better by combining the tools of scholarship with the virtues of humbly listening to the interpretations of others and above all to the Holy Spirit."[12]

Given the contingent (dependent) nature of our understandings, then, we begin to see that the idea that we are all walking around with the same understanding of God and the same version of the Christian faith that has always been around is simply a nice idea. Nice, but false. Even the early Christians struggled with interpretation and understanding.[13] The fact is that we are on a journey. A journey that sometimes feels like a high wire act. Rather than thinking of a net, then, as a list of "absolutes" or "essential doctrines," I would prefer to think of the net as God himself. We may take a misstep. We might even fall. That's part of what it means to be on a journey, and at some point we have to trust the Psalmist, who declares, "he will not let your foot slip," and "he will watch over your coming and going." Or we might say, our "slipping and falling." In light of that, I'd prefer the net to be God (or ultimate reality), rather than a net of our own making.

SETTING SAIL

I had the opportunity to go sailing recently with a friend. We sailed a forty-foot boat that was similar to a nineteenth-century English cutter, with traditional rigging. It took a lot of work and a number of us to be handling the mainsail, the foresail, the jib, and the ropes. It was a bit intimidating, particularly for those of us who had never sailed, or at least not on a boat

---

12. Ibid., 15.

13. See Acts 15 for one such example of Scriptural/contextual debate.

of that sort. Many of us had a lot to learn. What was interesting to me, though, was that even the two experienced sailors on the boat couldn't do it alone. They needed each of us to chip in. And so we were hoisting the sails, tying ropes, tacking, following instructions—and doing it together. It had to happen in community, and those of us who were novices were thankful for the more experienced sailors on board, and for a captain that had sailed many times.

Despite my initial trepidation, once we were out in the open water, and the breeze was whipping through our hair, the sunshine was bright upon us—what an experience! I have rarely felt so alive. I can see why so many are drawn to sailing. The combination of preparation, of know-how, of teamwork—everything involved—all pays off in the end, and it is a truly satisfying form of recreation. But the truth is, it's not for everyone. Some people have a genuine issue with sea-sickness. Some might prefer to zip around in a motorboat. Some prefer the steadiness of land to the unsteadiness and uncertainty of the open sea. This is all true. But does that mean that no one else should sail?

I wonder how this applies to spirituality. When it comes to the open seas of faith, are there uncharted waters yet to be discovered? Many would say, "No, there are not." Has the entire spiritual landscape already been discovered? Many would respond, "Yes, it has." I, along with others, would beg to differ. If God is as big as our religious traditions claim he is, I would guess we are only at the tip of the iceberg (OK, bad analogy to mix in with sailing). Some indeed may prefer the security of land to the unpredictability of the open seas. But isn't it in the open seas where new discovery happens? What if it is time to throw off the old moorings, or at least take a little dinghy out to explore?

The philosopher Emmanuel Levinas has said, "the other person is a shore we will never reach, another side for which we set sail in our little crafts but one on which we never actually arrive."[14] In other words, even in our closest relationships, such as with a very good friend or a spouse, there remains a distance that we can never close. There is a part of them that will always remain out of reach and unavailable to us. Even knowing this irreducible gap exists, we all probably agree that relationships are still worth having. If this is true of human relationships, how much more so of relationships to the Divine?

14. Quoted in Caputo, *What Would Jesus Deconstruct?*, 44.

I am reminded of the main character, Van Weyden, from Jack London's novel, *The Sea Wolf*. He is on a large vessel heading out to sea in the fog on the San Francisco Bay, and is reflecting on the scene:

> I fell to dwelling upon the romance of the fog. And romantic it certainly was—the fog, like the gray shadow of infinite mystery, brooding over the whirling speck of earth; and men, mere motes of light and sparkle, cursed with an insane relish for work, riding their steeds of wood and steel through the heart of the mystery, groping their way blindly through the Unseen, and clamoring and clanging in confident speech the while their hearts are heavy with incertitude and fear.[15]

What a terrific description of our lot as humanity—we are sailing through the universe amid a certain fog of unknowing. There is so much about our world that we simply don't know! Yet this has not prevented us from making dramatic declarations that we know far more than we actually do. Religion has often led the way in this unfounded certainty. Perhaps a bit more modesty about the extent of such knowledge, coupled with awe at the wonder around us and hope that we can ride this craft well together, would create for a better journey. So what of faith? Has it no place in this common journey? Must it be left on shore? On the contrary, I believe it has an important role to play. Faith, in this venture, would serve us better—not as harsh 'clanging speech'—but rather whispered words of hope and love, which, from time to time, may well put a little wind in our sails.

For some, the familiarity of base camp calls, the certainty of the dock beckons, and the platform, well, it's much preferable to the wire. At times we just want what is solid, firm, familiar. Yet perhaps it is time to get in the boat and unhook the moorings; time to step onto the high wire, and stop worrying about the net; time to put our boots on and set out for the climb. In my own experience, the hardest part generally precedes the really good parts. If we take the step, we might even find that we rather enjoy the breeze, the smell of the open sea, the possibility of new discovery, the adventure of the climb, and the view from up high.

15. London, *The Sea Wolf*, 3.

14

An Evolving Faith

As we live and grow, our beliefs change.
They must change.

—Martin Buber

THE LIFE CYCLE

My youngest child is finally leaving the diaper stage. This is not insignificant! She is our fourth child (three big brothers), and in some ways was easier to potty-train, and in some ways harder. She took steps in the right direction at an earlier age than her brothers did, but now, when we are nearly home-free, she is regressing. Some months earlier she wet her pants for the first time in quite a while. Our natural response was to throw her pants in the laundry and throw her in the bath tub. Simple enough. Well, not long after that initial incident, she wet her pants again.

"Josephine, you're a big girl now. Why did you pee in your pants again?"

She grinned at me: "Because I want to take a bath."

Well, when you've got a beautiful, curly-haired blonde little princess flashing her innocent grin at you, you're practically defenseless to do anything but what she asks.

"OK, Josephine, I'll put you in the tub—but you *cannot* pee your pants just to take a bath! If you want a bath, just ask."

An Evolving Faith   111

Well, let's just say we are still working on this step.

This transition is one among many. It is a helpful transition (if and when we get there), because the children are no longer dependent on me every time they need to "go." They take some ownership and begin to use the toilet for themselves. They are no longer dependent upon the diapers or training pants that were there to make sure they didn't make a mess all over. They have graduated to a new stage. (Unfortunately pointing to her big brothers standing up and going doesn't really help her.) But when children learn to use the bathroom on their own, they have taken a step toward independence (though there are many steps yet to take).

We grow and change physically. We adapt and change in regard to our environment. In the face of all these changes, many find comfort in something that is unchanging: their faith. It is the same now as it was when they were children. There is immense comfort in that. Yet I wonder if faith—one's approach to God and religious beliefs—is not that different than the changes we go through in life. We grow up, and that causes us to think differently, to acquire different attitudes and behave differently. This happens in one's relation to family, art, science, music, and politics. What if a healthy faith is one that grows and changes, just as we do? What if such a faith reflects the various stages we go through in life? When we are children, we are in a dependence stage. We need someone to feed us, bathe us, change us, take us places, and so on. Is a young faith in God very different? We rely upon God in similar ways. We expect God to do X, Y, and Z.

As we grow, we begin to realize that our parents can't do everything for us, indeed, we don't *want* them to do everything for us. Soon, we can feed ourselves, we can make our own lunches, we can get around on our own, whether by bicycle, driving, or even walking somewhere alone. Many things begin to change. Perhaps also when it comes to God, we begin to realize that God is like a parent—one who doesn't do everything for us, or hold our hand every step of the way. We grow up, we begin to take ownership of our lives, of our mistakes, of our responsibilities, and so on. A faith stuck in childhood might keep us from doing very much, because we are sitting around waiting for God to do it. I wonder if a growing faith perceives that God is there patiently encouraging us to grow up and do things for ourselves? This does not mean that God is not involved. It seems that at some underlying level we would continue to rely upon

God for strength and encouragement, even as we may do so in relation to our parents once we are out of the house and "on our own," so to speak.

I began to think about this idea as I read Philip Gulley's book, *The Evolution of Faith*. He too notes that he "wondered if our relationship with God mirrored our relationship with our parents, moving through the cycles of dependence, mutual friendship, and reciprocal assistance."[1] In other words, the stage of dependence happens when we are young, as we've already noted. A stage in which we look to God "primarily as a parental figure who can be trusted to provide for us and protect us from life's hazards."[2] He notes that this is a very child-like relationship, in which "God does for us what our parents did for us when we were children— God protects us, God provides for us, and though God could protect us from all harm, he is wiser than us and sometimes lets us experience pain so we might learn a lesson or later enjoy a greater good."[3] I think many, many people have such a relationship with God, and find extreme comfort in it. It was certainly true for much of my own faith journey. Gulley notes similarly that such a view enjoys a wide embrace, and that many will never transcend this theological stage of dependence. The benefits are many. We live in an unpredictable, changing world, and "a theology that asserts God's parental, unfailing care can be a strong comfort to those who suffer."[4] There is a downside, however. He notes that "the risk of this spiritual stasis is that people sometimes remain entrenched, mistaking fixed beliefs for faith, thinking other views of God are wrong, if not evil."[5] In other words, we may begin to become defensive about any other approach to God, and will dogmatically assert our own view as *the* view, and we will deflect attempts at re-examining such a faith approach too closely.

Let's go back to the parental connection. Ideally, our relationship with our parents changes over the years, as we grow and develop and become more independent. Many of us experience this transition in very similar ways. At a certain age, for most of us sometime shortly after high school, we move out on our own, either attending college or working full-time and earning enough to live on our own. This does not mean we no

1. Gulley, *The Evolution of Faith*, 125.
2. Ibid.
3. Ibid., 126.
4. Ibid.
5. Ibid.

longer are in relationship with our parents (hopefully!). Rather, it is a new stage. We still express our love to them, we still may remain dependent on them in some ways, but we have reached a new level. The expectation is that I will begin to take care of myself more and more.

But this shift is not easy, and not without ups and downs. There is a freedom that comes with independence, but also a certain amount of anxiety. Will I make it? Will I make the right decisions? Will I perhaps begin a family of my own at some point, and will I choose the right partner for that endeavor? These and many other questions are no longer answered for us—we must answer them for ourselves, even with the support and encouragement of our parents. If our parents were to make these decisions for us, most of us would begin to resent still being treated like a child. Many of us have come across people who have not had a healthy separation from their parents, and the result is an unhealthy dependence where the person is not able to function effectively on his or her own.

Gulley notes that his own faith began to shift around the same time his relationship with his parents shifted. He notes, "Previously I had viewed God as an all-powerful parental figure who regularly intervened to fix my problems. I had no hesitation asking God to involve herself in the minutiae of my life, providing one thing or another to make my life more pleasant."[6] This is the very kind of faith many of us are encouraged weekly to have, even as adults. Gulley's view was shifting: "I began to wonder whether God might be weary of my daily pleadings and might be expecting me to assume a larger share of duties, not only my own, but the duties of those unable to care for themselves."[7] Now many Christians would posit that one should do both: plead with God while also doing one's own part. I certainly commend this view, and practice it myself. Yet for Gulley, it was a sense that something was changing, and that "the key to my spiritual growth lay in my willingness and ability to become God's partner instead of God's child."[8]

Some Christians may think this borders on blasphemy, but this idea is nothing new, and is in fact an idea deeply rooted in Judaism as well as Christianity. This is something that has come up in our gatherings at the pub. The Jewish idea of *tikkun olam*, or healing the world, is precisely that

6. Ibid., 127.

7. Ibid.

8. Ibid., 128.

God is looking for partners in his overall redemptive plan. This is clearly echoed in many Christian traditions as well. Jesus tells his disciples that they will "do greater things than these," implying that we are expected to not only carry on his work, but that, perhaps collectively, we will do more than he was able to do individually.[9]

I had a conversation with a humanist friend lately who noted that the problem many non-believers (atheists, humanists, and others) have with people of faith is that they seem unwilling to grapple with the problems of our world because they continue on in their childlike assumption that God is going to take care of everything and therefore we don't need to worry about it. In other words, one's faith in God—particularly when it remains at a level of childish dependence—could be the very impediment to making real progress on the very real problems we all face together. He noted his gratitude in interfaith conversations and settings like Pub Theology, because they allowed him to see that not all people of faith had this approach.

My own approach on this has certainly shifted, thanks in part to my involvement in Pub Theology. There was a time in the evangelical zeal of my youth when I had a distorted view of the whole as well. A friend and I used to joke that whenever something was broken, or stolen, or when we ourselves mistreated something, that "Oh well, it's all gonna burn anyway." And we would laugh off the situation of brokenness rather than honestly seek to engage it in such a way as to bring healing and wholeness, or at the very least to grieve the brokenness. We might like to think that such a view is a distorted caricature that true people of faith do not have, but unfortunately it is out there more than we may realize. I have a friend who thinks that "recycling is stupid" because God is going to destroy the earth anyway. He is a deeply devout Christian, and is incredibly sincere about his faith. It seems to me that the key to helping our world move forward is not, as Sam Harris might prefer, to end faith, but rather to engage it in honest dialogue in settings such as Pub Theology and other interfaith gatherings.

So we've talked about faith developing along the similar lines of our relationship to our parents as we travel through the life cycle. Can we take this a little farther? What about when our parents reach an age where it becomes our turn to take care of them? This time is coming for me, and

9. John 14:12.

I have already seen it as my parents have cared for their own parents (my grandparents). Is it possible to think there is a time in our relationship with God that might reflect this earlier reversal of care? Philip Gulley thinks so. "God is no longer able to do for me, at least in my mind, what I once thought him capable of. Consequently, instead of viewing God as one who helps me accomplish my purposes, it is now my job to help God accomplish the divine purpose—seeking the best for others and seeking the growth of the beloved, which is to say, everyone."[10]

THE WEAKNESS OF GOD

Some of you are cringing at the thought of this presumption. God as a weakling? God needing our help? You may be thinking: I believe in a God of power, a God who can do anything! Yet I wonder if that reflects more upon the faith of your childhood, rather than your actual experience of God in the world. Some would say that a biblical perspective may indeed reveal that God, rather than being an overpowering enforcer of his will, acts rather as a weak force in the world. Does not the very season of Advent and the celebration of the child in the manger speak to a God who was willing to become weak and entirely dependent upon others?

Theologian Jacques Ellul notes that this is true of the grown Jesus in some sense as well: "What constantly marked the life of Jesus was not nonviolence per se, but in every situation the choice not to use power."[11] It seems to me that a proper theology of the cross is a theology not of power, but of weakness.

In his book, *The Weakness of God*, John Caputo says, "The weak force of God is to lay claim upon us—not the way a sovereign power invades and then lays claim to territory, overpowers its native population and plants a foreign flag, but in the way of a summons that calls and provokes, an appeal that incites or invites us, a promise that awakens our love."[12] God, in the Christian tradition, doesn't overpower us and say, "You *will* believe in me!" but rather lays down his life on our behalf, thereby becoming powerless in a display of love that proves to be irresistible to many people. That includes me.

10. Gulley, *Evolution of Faith*, 128.

11. Ellul, *What I Believe*, 147.

12. Caputo, *The Weakness of God*, 38.

This God is present in our world precisely in such a way that *requires* us to be the very agents by which he accomplishes his purposes. I tend to see this as a marked improvement over theologies of certainty and agendas of power.

Gulley concludes his chapter on comparing his own faith journey to the life cycle as follows: "When I was young, God was my parent figure. As I moved into independence, I viewed God as my partner, and I experienced a mutuality of friendship and responsibility I had never before felt. I wonder if the next step is a return to total dependence on God as I age and weaken, or further independence as my growth in wisdom hopefully accompanies my growth in age."[13] This is Gulley's experience, and he is using an analogy to help describe it. Some of you will identify with it. Others of you will not. There are obvious disanalogies: our parents grow old and feeble, we change in many ways, etc. We should not confuse ourselves with God. We don't grow up and become divine beings, neither does God grow old and feeble. The above idea of the weakness of God is rather that God often chooses to act as a weak force in the world.[14] The analogy works well when it focuses on our own perception and understanding of God and how that changes, just as we change in many other ways in our lives.

My own faith, as it has grown and developed in a setting like Pub Theology, has similarly shifted, changed, grown, and developed. More and more I realize that in my own faith I, too, need to grow up in some ways and be more independent. In other ways I find I am increasingly dependent—not only on God, but on others. I need others—their insights, experiences, prayers, spiritual practices, wisdom, and care. Perhaps a return to dependence in our life of faith is not a step back, but a step forward. Was this not also the experience God himself had in the incarnation?

STAGES OF FAITH

Faith changes, adapts, and matures over time. Lack of change would seem to indicate lack of growth. And what is not growing is generally considered not alive. Another way to frame the growth and development of faith that is helpful for many of us involved in Pub Theology has been articulated by James Fowler, modeled on Lawrence Kohlberg's stages of

13. Gulley, *The Evolution of Faith*, 128.

14. Though Caputo would go farther and say that is *the* way God works in the world.

moral development. It is a chart of spiritual growth in some ways similar to Gulley's life cycle approach. He calls it the "Stages of Faith." These can be summarized as: 1) Intuitive-Projective Faith (infancy and early childhood); 2) Mythic-Literal Faith (early childhood to adolescence); 3) Synthetic-Conventional Faith (adolescence to early adulthood); 4) Individuative-Reflective Faith (twenties to forties); 5) Conjunctive Faith (forties and beyond); 6) Universalizing Faith. Fowler notes, "We all begin the pilgrimage of faith as infants."[15]

The first stage is the "fantasy-filled, imitative phase in which the child can be powerfully and permanently influenced by examples, moods, actions and stories of the visible faith of . . . adults."[16] In other words, this age perceives the world through a lens of imagination and intuition unrestrained by logic. It is a time when one lives in a magical world in which anything is possible.

Stage two is the stage in which "the person begins to take on for himor herself the stories, beliefs and observances that symbolize belonging to his or her community. Beliefs are appropriated with literal interpretations, as are moral rules and attitudes."[17] The gift of this stage is narrative. Children love a good story, and the child begins to learn to absorb and retell powerful stories that grasp his or her experiences of meaning. There is a quality of literalness about this. The child is not yet ready to step outside the stories and reflect upon their meanings. The child takes symbols and myths at pretty much face value, though they may touch or move him or her at a deeper level. Here one sees the world as a story—concrete, literal, narrative family of ritual and myth, e.g., "In the beginning, God created the . . ."

The third stage, notes Fowler, typically has its rise in adolescence, but "for many adults, it becomes a permanent place of equilibrium."[18] For many it is a "conformist" stage in the sense that it is "acutely tuned to the expectations and judgments of significant others" and "as yet does not have a sure enough grasp on its own identity . . . to construct and maintain an independent perspective." One of the hallmarks of this stage is that it tends to compose its images of God as extensions of interpersonal

15. Fowler, *Stages of Faith*, 119.

16. Ibid., 133.

17. Ibid., 149.

18. Ibid., 172.

relationships. God is often experienced as a friend, in a relationship in which one is known deeply and valued. Many people, in churches and out, are best described by faith that essentially took form when they were adolescents. The name "conventional" means that most people in this stage see themselves as believing what "everybody else" believes and would be reluctant to stop believing it because of the need they feel to stay connected with their group. It turns out that most of the people in traditional churches are at this stage. And in fact, Fowler comes right out and states that religious institutions "work best" if the majority of their congregation is in Stage 3. (Now that explains a lot of the preaching we hear that sounds destined to discourage people from questioning! To properly assure their continuance, churches apparently need people to remain in Stage 3.) When a person cognitively realizes that there are contradictions between some of his authority sources and is ready to actually reflect realistically on them, he or she begins to be ready to move to the fourth stage.

Stage four is a critical point. It is a transition in which the person "must begin to take seriously the burden of responsibility for his or her own commitments, lifestyle, beliefs and attitudes."[19] The strength of this stage is that one gains the capacity for critical reflection. This is primarily a stage of angst and struggle, in which one must face difficult questions regarding identity and belief. This is a stage of de-mythologizing, where what was once unquestioned is now subjected to critical scrutiny. Stage four is heavily existential and disillusionment reigns. This stage is not a comfortable place to be and, although it can last for a long time, those who stay in it do so in danger of becoming bitter, suspicious characters who trust nothing and no one. But most, after entering this stage, sense that not only is the world far more complex than his or her stage three mentality would allow for, it is still more complex and numinous than the agnostic rationality of stage four allows.

Stage five is when one begins to reclaim and rework one's past. It is in this stage that one "chooses regression in the service of transcendence." It is a time when one develops a "second naivete" when "symbolic power is reunited with conceptual meanings."[20] Here one moves from stage four's rationalism to the acknowledgement of paradox and transcendence. It was Karl Barth and Paul Ricoeur's common conviction that theological

19. Ibid., 182.
20. Ibid., 197.

interpretation of the Bible ought to lead us beyond a critical preoccupation with the text to a fresh encounter with the divine reality to which the text bears witness.[21] In this stage a person grasps the reality behind the symbols of his or her inherited systems, and is also drawn to an acknowledging of the symbols of others' systems. People in this stage are willing to engage in dialogue with those of other faiths in the belief that they might learn something that will allow them to correct their own truths. To get to this point, it is critical that the person has moved through the demythologizing phase of stage four. This stage makes room for mystery and the unconscious, and is fascinated by it while at the same time apprehensive of its power. It sees the power behind the metaphors while simultaneously acknowledging their relativity. In stage five, the world is re-sacralized, literally brimming with vision, or as Rob Bell would say: "Everything is spiritual." It is also imbued with a new sense of justice that goes beyond justice defined by one's own culture and people.

The final stage, according to Fowler, is reached only by the very, very few. Examples Fowler names are Gandhi, Martin Luther King, Jr., and Mother Teresa.[22] In a sense we can describe this stage as one in which persons begin radically to live as though what Christians and Jews call the "kingdom of God" were already a fact. These people experience a shift from the self as the center of experience. Now their center becomes a participation in God or ultimate reality. We experience these people on the one hand as being more lucid and simple than we are, and on the other hand as intensely liberating people, sometimes even subversive in their liberating qualities.

We could certainly debate these stages and how accurate they are. Are they descriptive or prescriptive? Do they happen in this linear fashion? Do they happen at all? But regardless of these models, it seems to me that if faith is truly a living reality, it will grow and change. This is inevitable. Perhaps there has been some change in your own faith journey. My own has been helped inestimably by have a setting like Pub Theology where I can share my doubts, voice my questions, and have my certainties unmasked. A place where people at all stages are welcome. It is not easy ground to tread, but how much better to tread in community than alone? Some face this very reality.

21. Ibid.
22. Ibid., 201.

A while back I wrote a blog post summarizing these six stages of faith. The post was helpful for many, including a reader from Seattle named Andrew. After reading my post, he responded with the following:

> If you can stage my life to simplify it, I'm going through stage 4 right now after my life was completely shattered by those I was on the "in" with. It is such a struggle because I constantly feel the pressure to go back to conforming and being a part of the group I once was a part of because I feel so left out. And considering my family is trying to save me from myself and this time of deconstruction in my life, and absolutely afraid that I'm walking away from the "faith," this time of my life is so very hard and I don't feel encouragement but only a deep sense of failure from those who say they love me (practically, everyone).
>
> Every day I ask myself, "What is love?" because I'm constantly barraged with Scripture verses from others trying to convince me that my questions and doubts are unbiblical, and that God really has all this anger and wrath stored up for me (and everyone else) unless I believe in certain doctrines; and because of this, the most loving thing to do is to save me from my deceptive self regardless of how I feel about it. But I feel in my heart this deep desire for real love and I honestly don't want to be a part of something that does things out of fear. I just see a different definition of love from most Christians that doesn't feel like love at all.
>
> Anyway, thank you for your authentic questions and words of encouragement. I'm finding encouragement from men like Peter Rollins as well. But it's so hard to go through this time in my life feeling alone in the faith because I fear every Christian around me. I don't feel loved by them at all, and it scares me because I want to love God, but I don't want to be like every Christian around me who seems to be (deep down, even if they don't want to admit it) motivated by a fear of hell or punishment from God. I know it's not every Christian, but it feels like it because I feel like I haven't met one with real love in their eyes and not just a love they claim with their lips.

Andrew was growing in his faith, perhaps even entering a new and difficult phase. But those who should have been near him encouraging and supporting him, were instead allowing his growth to become a source of anxiety for themselves, thus they responded by opposing his own shifting faith experience. A setting like Pub Theology could have been the very thing needed—that place both safe and unsafe, where he would be accepted and allowed the space needed for his faith to work itself out.

I think by now you've gotten the idea that the best evidence for faith in someone's life is not simple and slavish devotion to a body of dogma. Ironically, that may exhibit a profound lack of faith. Rather, I am expounding the idea that one's faith ought to grow, change, and develop, just as a person physically, emotionally, and intellectually grows, changes, and develops. Yet some will continue to resist the idea that faith changes or grows, because they will claim to hold to the faith "once delivered, for all the saints." But this is to again mistake the content of faith for the experience of faith, or how one appropriates and understands that content. Certainly faith rests on both content and experience, but we often confuse the former with the latter.

An ideal faith life, as far as I can tell, is not one that maintains the same ideas and approaches as when one was a child. A faith journey that never leaves home, that stays rooted in childlike certainties, might well be easier and simpler, but it is not one that will likely render healthy fruit in the long run. I think the church has historically had moments where it truly helped people develop their faith, but in many other cases—as noted with Andrew—it has opposed true faith development in the name of defending dogma. Can the church be a place to foster such growth today? I think so, and it may not be the sanctuary where such growth happens—it may well be in living rooms, coffee shops, and yes, even pubs.

15

Tapping into Theology

The words printed here are concepts. You must go through the experiences.

—Saint Augustine

Hey, careful, man, there's a beverage here!

—The Dude, *The Big Lebowski*

GO FOR IT

My hope throughout this project has been to give you a taste of what our gatherings at the pub are like, and how it has impacted a few of us who have been involved. Through these pages you've been given a seat at the table, so to speak. What would encourage me greatly is if this experience has sparked a small desire in you to seek out and learn from those who are quite different from you. No doubt some readers have already set the book down chapters ago, with the intent of contacting me personally to correct my theology and misconceptions. That's OK. I invite the conversation. Perhaps others of you will realize that there is value in what we are doing, and that it's maybe even something you can do as well.

If that is you—this chapter will attempt to give some basic pointers. The first thing is this: it doesn't have to look exactly like our gathering. In fact, I would recommend it doesn't. It should be tailored to your own community and reflect your own style. It doesn't have to be at a pub or a brewery. It doesn't have to include beer. I have heard of groups like "Theology Over Pizza" and "Coffee and Doubt" that are doing many of the same things we are. It doesn't even have to be a formal gathering. What would make me the most satisfied is to have a reader or two who, having ventured this far, will begin to see the surprising diversity around them, not as a threat, but as an opportunity. An opportunity not to evangelize, but to learn.

A pastor from Montana sent me a note a while back to let me know that his own community was attempting something similar to Pub Theology.

"We started what we call 'Theology and Coffee' once a month, on a Sunday evening at a local restaurant. We have gotten some from our church and some other Christians from the community, but we really haven't been able to attract the unbelievers and skeptics. Any ideas?"

I was encouraged to hear of his community's efforts. He is one of a number of pastors and others who have contacted me with similar questions. This is something that is catching on with people, and I think that is only going to increase. So what to do? No one likes to throw a party and have no one show up. What would you suggest?

My initial thought was that perhaps coffee on Sunday night felt too much like church to some people. Maybe what seemed a neutral location to members of his church was actually a bit of a comfort zone, and would have different connotations for others. Setting may seem like a minor thing, but you have to be somewhere that is comfortable for people, *somewhere they might be hanging out anyway.* And the environment has to be conducive to your gathering. If it's a more formal restaurant, or a place where people primarily come for dinner, it may be awkard for a group to be sitting around trying to get deep over coffee. Setting matters—be sure you are in an inviting, comfortable atmosphere.

My second thought was to consider who his community was inviting—perhaps they had not actually invited anyone other than friends of the same background. I suggested that they make an effort to get to know some people who were not Christians, if they did not have such friends already. If you don't know any atheists, agnostics, Buddhists, or others, it's hard to invite them. I suggested that they drop by a local humanist group or free thought society.

My final thought was that maybe they hadn't advertised adequately. A good way to get the word out is putting a note in local newspapers and weeklies, to put up posters in places like coffee shops, and certainly at the venue you are gathering at. Perhaps they have a schedule of regular events. Get on that schedule! Of course, personal invitations and word of mouth buzz are the best. In the end, I congratulated him on their efforts, and encouraged him to keep after it. Sometimes good things take time to get off the ground.

This group's struggles made me begin to wonder—what makes such a gathering work? How is it that we've had the success we've had, and the amount of diversity represented, especially considering the size of our town?

There are many intangibles, and we tried to follow the above methods: invite a diverse audience, have a good setting, get the word out. Perhaps there is something about the setting that is crucial. Maybe a pub setting really is ideal. David, one of our regular attenders, feels this way:

"The whole idea of having beer sets the tone. It says, 'This is a social gathering. This is a group of regular people. Pretense is at a minimum. It is not going to be churchy.' And of course, in addition to the idea of beer is the beer itself; it doesn't hurt because it lowers one's inhibitions and allows one to speak a bit freer than one might in other, more formal settings."

I honestly think he's on to something. Certainly alcohol is not required, but for many people, a neighborhood bar is a place they are accustomed to going for relaxation and conversation. A restaurant potentially is seen as simply a place one goes to eat. If there are not other groups of people just hanging out and talking, it may not be the proper ambience. Now, no one is to say this can't happen over coffee or diet Cokes. It can. In fact, I have a friend who pulls off a similar gathering at a coffee shop he calls "Coffee and Doubt." Apparently it works. So the point is—know your community and where the gathering spots are, call it what you want, get the word out, and go for it.

WHO'S IN CHARGE HERE?

Maybe you're worried about who is going to lead the thing. What if someone asks a question I don't have the answer to? What if the conversation gets out of control? Perhaps you're wondering what my role is as the pastor and as the quote-unquote "leader" of the group. Do I pause graciously while others are talking, holding my wisdom until the conversation falls silent, awaiting my chance to enlighten everyone with my wisdom? By now you realize I do nothing of the sort.

Rather than being an answer man, I ask questions. Rather than dominate, I attempt to facilitate. Minimally. As already noted, I bring a list of questions, topics and poems or quotes—usually 5 or 6 with the intention that these are merely a springboard for the conversation. Shaping where the conversation goes is not necessarily my intention with bringing the topics. We simply need to start somewhere, and bringing the topics is for the purpose of getting us talking. If you recall, at our initial gathering we did not have topics, and we all kind of sat around looking at each other like, "So what should we talk about?" It may help to have one of the topics, particularly one of the first ones, be something easy, and something everyone can contribute to. For example, we might ask, "What is your favorite season and why?" or "Name something awesome." It breaks the ice and gets people involved. For some built-in diversity, you may want to include quotes from people of all perspectives—religious, non-religious, from rabbis and mullahs, from priests and pagans. We have a decent amount of religious diversity in our area, but definitely a Christian majority. Yet we have had Jews, Muslims, Buddhists, Hindus, Wiccans, agnostics, atheists, and others at the table—not bad for a small town in Northern Michigan. How much diversity is in your area? Probably more than you realize.

An important role of being facilitator is making sure that no one person hijacks the conversation. Some people will come who have an agenda and want to clearly steer the conversation in one certain direction —you will want to have, or be, a person who is able to gently and tactfully keep the conversation open to the whole group.

Another challenge is keeping a certain level of depth to the conversation, without plunging to levels that are incoherent to most people. There have been times where we've gone to depths that only allow one or two people at the table to participate or even follow what is being said. That may be helpful on occasion, giving everyone a chance to learn something, but can become tiresome when the majority of the group feels left out. Sometimes I bring an obscure quote from a medieval theologian or a contemporary philosopher, and only a few of us at the table are able to comprehend what was said. Perhaps this is a mistake, but I think as long as it can be explained to everyone, that it is good for people to feel like there is some learning they have to do about theology and philosophy. We are in general a very shallow culture when it comes to deep, meaningful theological thinking. We take what we can get on the religion channel or off the shelf at the bookstore—which is often comprised of "pop theology" or "theology lite," such as "Does Jesus Want You To Succeed?" or "How I Died and Went to Heaven — and So Can You!," or the like.

There is certainly a place for this, and we are not trying to be so esoteric that only PhDs can join our conversation—but we are trying to help people realize that there is incredible depth to the topics we are discussing. Even if our particular conversation never reaches the depth of the quote we are discussing, it whets the appetite to explore these things further, to read about these topics, to come back for more conversation. It is an art trying to balance conversation at a more popular level with conversation that is more academic and less accessible.

Some folks show up at our pub gatherings who expect that it is going to be more or less a Sunday school-ish discussion, the only difference being that we are drinking beer instead of bad church coffee. They expect topics like, "How can Jesus help my marriage?" Or, "What does the Bible have to say about raising kids?" They are usually disappointed. It is not a self-help group—though many find great help in being there, and we do discuss practical, on-the-ground implications of what is being discussed. (This increases even more as relationships and friendships develop within the group, leading to an increased willingness to be open.) But we generally begin somewhere else, knowing that if our theoretical framework for something needs adjusting, that will be important to attend to initially, and may well help put the practical on the right footing.

Our topics tend to be more like, "Who was Jesus? Explain the difference between Jesus of Nazareth and Jesus Christ," and the direction of the conversation will be more like, "He was a first-century peasant, as best we can tell, who was considered to be a holy man or prophet, who had some followers, and was executed by Rome." An ensuing discussion on Christological development in the early church will likely break out, or on the historical reliability of the Gospels, whether or not non-canonical books like the Gospel of Thomas ought to inform our perspectives on Jesus, or how we are to grapple with and hold various perspectives on Jesus today. Eventually we may come around to—given the various perspectives at the table—what it might look like for someone to follow this Jesus.

Those coming with a tract to convince everyone of one perspective on Jesus are certainly welcome to give that perspective, but will be sorely disappointed if the group does not end with a stamp of approval on that particular stance, or declares that there is no "official" Pub Theology stance on that question (or any other question!). This is extremely difficult and challenging for many Christians. Some of you may even be wincing as you read this.

"So, aren't you just opening up the door to a bunch of gobbledy-gook and theological hodge-podge?"

"Are you just mish-mashing everything together and saying everyone and everything is OK?"

Yes.

Yes to the extent that everyone, regardless of his or her perspective is OK. Yes, to the extent that people are allowed to hold whatever view they want to hold. Yes, to the extent that the first step in anyone changing their opinion on anything is feeling a safe place to state what it is they believe now. Do I have my own opinions on who Jesus was/is? Of course. I wouldn't be a Christian, let alone a pastor, otherwise. Will I state that? Yes, as my opinion, based on my own theological tradition and understanding, but I will not state that it is the official opinion of Pub Theology or the one perspective everyone *must* hold or they are not allowed to be there. The latter approach would do more to drive people away than cause them to consider my perspective. There is nothing wrong with stating your convictions and beliefs flat out. In fact, you should. But such things must be said with tact, with grace, and with the humility that says, "but I could be wrong about that."

In the end, my role as facilitator is to ask good questions which provoke and encourage discussion, to listen well, to reflect back to people what they are saying, perhaps to reframe someone's input so that the rest of the group can be sure they heard it clearly, and to allow the speaker the encouragement to know that we hear what he or she is saying. If there are pauses I can keep the conversation going with a good question or provocative statement. You may choose to operate differently, but this approach has worked well for us.

HOSPITALITY

One thing to always remember is that for many people, showing up at a place they've maybe never been and meeting new people to discuss intensely personal topics can be a very difficult thing to do. One of the keys to making this work is helping people feel welcomed. It is easy for any group that meets with any regularity to start feeling closed, that is, only the regulars are welcome, and newcomers aren't. A conversational group at the pub is no different. So how do you do this?

Well, the most obvious one is having a sign up letting people know you are meeting that night, and where to find you in the bar. Despite the fact that it seems easier to join a discussion about God at a pub than show up as a stranger at a church on a Sunday morning—in some ways, the latter allows for some anonymity that the former does not. Here, you have to introduce yourself, and you may well be asked for your opinion. Show up at your average church and at most you have to shake a couple hands. Other than that you are allowed to worship in peace and participate at your own discretion. Despite the idea of "going where people are" and making it easier for people to attend, it can actually be a bit daunting for people to go up to a group of strangers in a bar with the topic of religion at hand. So it helps to have some good signs up, and it also helps if the bartenders are aware of the group's location so that they can direct any inquirers to the right table(s).

And it may seem a small thing, but always introduce yourself when newcomers join the table, and don't be afraid to pause the conversation to allow others to get in, and to briefly get them up to speed on the conversation. Another consideration is how large the group is. We have found that a very comfortable conversation can take place among ten or perhaps even a dozen people, but that when you get 15–20 or more people, you will likely have to divide into several groups. Another important way to keep the group open is to be sure to introduce everyone when new people are present, to make people feel welcome, to ask them about their own lives before launching a theological salvo their way.

It may be tempting, as conversation is going on, to refer to a prior week's discussion, or to use insider jargon that minimizes the ability of newcomers to engage in the conversation. Perhaps a deep discussion has occurred on a similar topic in recent weeks. It is unfair to assume someone knows all the ins and outs of what was discussed, and it may be best—for the sake of all involved—to at some level rehash some of the discussion, or at least build your point properly without assuming the foundations or prior discussion that was had for it to make sense in the present conversation.

Nancy is one of our regulars. Though she would mildly protest this, she is one of the elders of the group, in terms of age, life experience, and wisdom. She is a retired clergy member, who has found life in these conversations at the pub. One of the ways she expresses her gratitude and joy over this is to bring snacks. The pub lets you bring in your own food, so she brings in almonds, trail mix, pretzels, and the occasional bag of Doritos. And she brings plenty. It's a small gesture, but one that helps make newcomers welcome, and—hey—if we hit an awkward pause and no one has anything to contribute, you can always say, "Pass the peanuts."

You might think these are small, unimportant things. And perhaps they are. However, when you are dealing with issues that are so important to people, and so potentially volatile, you can't work hard enough to create a welcome, respectful atmosphere where people can trust the situation enough to engage in discussion about such things. Some people will come and not say a word the entire discussion. We never try to put someone on the spot. Sometimes a person will need to come for several weeks in a row or more before they feel comfortable or confident enough to jump into the discussion. The point is, as long as people have been in existence, they've had theological concerns, and they haven't always agreed. This disagreement can easily spill into antagonism, and from there it isn't a stretch to demonize a person and see her as an enemy. One thing that gives me great hope is that more and more these differences are being discussed in settings like ours, where the possibility of not only understanding but friendship is a real likelihood. Theological concerns are all around us—tap into them!

ON THE HOUSE

A couple years back we were approaching the anniversary of our first night of doing our pub discussions. One year of Pub Theology went by in a flash. Should we celebrate? Does anyone care? Is it corny to acknowledge this achievement? We decided to go for it. Why not? It was an experimental effort, this gathering at the pub and talking about God over beer, and it could have gone completely wrong. It could have ended in fights, in shouting matches, in someone spilling his beer on someone else. But none of that had happened. What happened instead was delightful. We had actually stumbled onto something. Something that was meeting a need for many of us—a safe, inviting place where we were welcome to ask our questions, voice our fears, acknowledge our frustrations and doubts, and above all, to learn from those who saw the world differently. On top of all of that, we had made some friends along the way. So celebrate we did.

We were going to buy a beer for everyone at the bar that night, but then figured we might find ourselves with some sort of liability we didn't want—imagine, a church buying beers for everyone. Actually I thought it was a good idea, but the pub owner told us to rethink it.

"Why don't you buy everyone some chips and hummus, or popcorn?"

"You sure? I really wanted to buy everyone a beer, or at least give everyone happy hour prices."

"People will take advantage."

"That's OK."

"I don't think so—it could get crazy. Let's stick with snacks."

We did snacks. I think he was right. The pub doesn't serve any food other than these light snacks, but some garlic hummus with locally made tortilla chips serves as a nice companion to a local microbrew. Any patrons at the pub that night were offered a free snack, courtesy of Pub Theology.

A number of people came by our table that night and said, "Thanks!" A few pulled up chairs and joined us. It wasn't anything flashy. Nothing big. But it helped make us a part of the happenings there at this particular brewery. We were on the schedule of weekly events. People expected us to be there—bartenders, regulars at the bar, pub theology seekers. It was nice to realize that people saw us as an expected fixture in their weeks—even if they didn't actually sit down at the table. They knew that if they had a question, or wanted to learn something about God or the Bible or philosophy, they could ask one of us, or simply pull up a chair and listen. And that's what it's all about.

16

Last Call

Everything has been figured out. Except how to live.

—Jean-Paul Sartre

ENCOUNTERING GOD EVERYWHERE

I love Pub Theology. I love Thursday nights. I love that I always learn something new. I love that I get to meet new people. People who grew up in different situations than I did. People who think differently. People who have different perspectives, who have studied different things, who follow different religious traditions, who've asked questions I haven't asked, who have been places I haven't been.

When this whole thing began, I felt pretty confident in my spiritual life, pretty sure I knew what I needed to know, and that if anything, those who showed up at those early Pub Theology gatherings would be fortunate to have the chance to hear me enlighten them. But the longer we've been doing this (we're in our fourth year now), the more I realize that often I am the one who needs to learn! To some, it would be heresy to think that I have anything to learn from a Buddhist, or an atheist, or a Muslim. But the truth is, there are many things to learn from such folks, and there are times where they will learn from me.

What if we approached people of other faiths or those without faith with a spirit of openness rather than fear? What if we approached others with a sincere desire to learn from them? One of my main contentions in this book is that Christians—at least in the West—have had the floor for long enough. We have controlled the conversation about God. We have set the parameters for spiritual pursuits. We have attempted to shut down dissenting voices and other approaches to God. The truth is, many are tired of this approach, and are beginning to look elsewhere for spiritual nourishment. Ironically, it may well be that opening ourselves up to the traditions of others is the very thing that helps save our own.

Barbara Brown Taylor notes that one of her own students—who is the son of a minister, no less—finds the Tibetan Buddhist dharma of compassion more compelling than the Christian law of love. Another has become a Wiccan, and a third has said that he has discovered more community in his weekly AA meeting than he ever felt in church.[1] By constantly seeking to control, we have squeezed people out of the picture—and they aren't standing for it anymore. If we refuse to recognize the merit in these other spiritual approaches, if we refuse to give respect to all people, regardless of their beliefs or lack thereof, we will no longer be respected in return.

And the truth is, we live in an increasingly global world, and our own neighborhoods are increasingly pluralistic. With the Internet and easy availability of books, we know more about other world religions than we ever have. Taylor notes as much: "His holiness the Dalai Lama has written books on the New York Times bestseller list. You may join a [virtual] ashram on the World Wide Web, or request materials from the International Society for Krishna Consciousness. You may take a class in Hatha Yoga or Tai Chi at your local YMCA, or join a transcendental meditation group sponsored by followers of the Maharishi Mahesh Yogi."[2]

In other words, the faiths of the world are now around us, whether we wish to acknowledge this or not. We can ignore them, or refuse to learn about them, but Taylor notes that "then you will not have anything very intelligent to say when someone asks you to help her think through the differences between the Buddha's Four Noble Truths and Jesus' Sermon on the Mount, or wants to know why Islam and Judaism agree that Christianity is not a monotheistic religion."[3] In other words,

1. Taylor, *Speaking of Sin*, 23.
2. Ibid., 24.
3. Ibid., 25.

you won't know how someone else perceives you if you don't take the time to get to know them. If you don't know how they perceive you, you will make wrong assumptions and communication becomes difficult. If you are trying to explain the Trinity to a Muslim friend, it might be helpful to know that many Muslims conceive of this as Father, Mother, and Son. Further, if you can't bother to be interested in learning about another person's approach to God, why should they be interested in yours?

Here we must be careful. We can begin to tip our toe over the line that says, I'm only going to listen to what you have to say as a formality, so that then you will give me the floor and I can tell you my story. This is disingenuous, and will be perceived as such. This may, in fact, be what happens if you show an interest in someone, but it should not be the motivation. The motivation should be because you care about getting to know someone. Because you have genuine interest in her approach to life, her perceptions about life and God and faith. Taylor notes that "the more we learn about other traditions, the more we learn about our own. It is helpful, for instance, since Jesus was a Jew, to know that Judaism has no doctrine of original sin, and that salvation is conceived of as life lived in obedience to Torah. Heaven and hell have never been very lively concepts for most Jews, who find the Christian focus on the world to come more than a little irrelevant. The point of human life on earth, as any son or daughter of Torah can tell you, is to assist God in the redeeming of this world now."[4]

When we approach the religious "other" with a spirit of respect and honest inquiry, we might be surprised at the wonderful things we learn. Things that can move us along the path in our own spiritual journey. When we approach them from a place of condescension, our own path becomes that much darker, our own approach that much smaller, and our faith that much less attractive to others. "The more adamant we are about God, the less likely we are to embody the traits we believe God values—love, compassion, peace, wisdom and patience."[5] In other words, in our efforts to refute other perspectives, to shout the loudest, to make sure people know that we are right, we may in fact be betraying the very God we are seeking to represent.

4. Ibid.
5. Gulley, *The Evolution of Faith*, 18.

The time has come to acknowledge that God is bigger than the Bible, that faith is not something Christians have a corner on, and that we may well encounter God in places we haven't been looking—in the humble submission of a Muslim, in the serenity of a Buddhist, in the commitment to Torah of a Jew, in the love of science and critical thinking of an atheist. Don't know any such people? Look them up. God won't mind. I promise.

WHERE IS THIS GOING?

Some will ask: "What is the point of all this discussion? Is it leading you closer to God? Is it leading others closer to God?" Those are good questions, and valid concerns for a person of faith. My own conviction is that each person is created in the image of God. As such, it stands to reason that each person has something of God in them, and something to teach me about God.

One regular at our gatherings, Steve, is a staunch atheist. He flat out doesn't believe in God. He's been attending our gatherings at the pub for over three years. If I had to wager, I would guess that Steve will never come to a place of belief in God. Some would say that perhaps he should stop coming. That maybe I should encourage him to join other discussions if he's not going to "get on board" with faith. There is a mentality in certain circles that someone is only worth spending time with if they come around to seeing things our way. Why continue to put energy into someone who doesn't get it?

Let's think about that for a second. Someone is only worth my time if they believe in God? Or more precisely, if they believe in the God I believe in? It seems to me that the very way of Jesus is to spend time with anyone, simply because they are a fellow human being, and that perhaps I am especially called to spend time with those who are often outcast by our communities of faith. Is Steve not worth befriending because he doesn't have my faith? If that's a position faith leads on to, I'd prefer to lump myself in with the atheists. The facts are that we are all human beings, and the minute we begin to denigrate others or see them as beneath us or not worth our time, perhaps our faith isn't worth having anymore. The reality is that I continue to learn from Steve things about life, about making the world a better place, about human relationships, about science fiction (Steve's an aficionado). I'm glad he's around, and consider him a good friend, and his faith or lack thereof has nothing to do with it.

The reality is that religious diversity is growing everywhere—and a forum like this creates a place for positive, respectful interaction, and the ability to learn from each other. All of this creates positive momentum in a community and the chance to work together for the common good, rather than seeing one another as opponents who need to be drawn into our own religious circle. In fact, through Pub Theology I was connected with an interfaith group that was just springing up in our area—the Area Council On Religious Diversity (ACORD)—which has subsequently hosted events like the afore-mentioned Tax Day Faith (or No Faith) Prayer and Meditation Breakfast. We invited city leaders and the community at large to gather and use prayers or positive thoughts from their faith (or nonfaith) tradition about wise use of tax dollars by our local, state and federal governments. It was a very positive event, despite the pushback mentioned in the introduction. Attendees represented several different faith traditions, as well as some people who did not subscribe to any religion.

REACTIONS

You've heard a lot from me. But here's what a few other folks have had to say:

"It is a wonderful work of inspiration, and I'm grateful it exists. Thank you for your foresight and custody of its creation. The very opportunity to discuss anything of import was a bit of heretofore withheld nourishment for me, and I hadn't been aware anything like this was going on. I look forward to attending again soon!"

"Just wanted you to know Steve and I were really glad that we stumbled onto Pub Theology a few weeks back. I can't imagine anything making robust theological conversation better than beer. Schedule permitting, hopefully one of these days I'll be able to come back."—Troy

"That was a lot of fun Bryan, even though we may not have answered all the questions on the list."—Nancy

"Reading [about Pub Theology], I have to tell you that I thought it was just spot on, and I thought that I would take some time and let you know. Pub Theology. To me, that sounds like going out into the world and bringing Jesus to where people are. That has an entirely different feel to it than inviting people to come onto our turf."

"Hi Bryan – I think it's a great place to have non-threatening, meaningful discussions with friends of all faiths. I have had many late-into-the evening discussions at our local watering hole with my non-Christian friends and have found them to be a real blessing. I appreciate also the courage to use the pub as your meeting place. Not everyone will agree that this is a good place to meet and you may receive some 'constructive criticism' from some for doing so but for many of us it's a natural comfortable place to meet. I applaud your approach."—Bernie

"I enjoyed participating in the Pub Theology discussion last evening at Right Brain Brewery. I greatly support interfaith dialogue, and was impressed at the number of folks attending last night's session, the gender balance in evidence, and the genuine interest and open sharing at our table. It was well worth the time spent."—Harry

"I think you'll be seeing me around on Thursday nights. What a great idea. Beer, conversation and God: three of my favorite things!"

"We had a great time and look forward to more! This is a great idea—we'll see you there again."

"Pub Theology breaks down the walls we all put up and confronts the snap judgments we can make—and I think that is true for all involved who understand the spirit of the gathering. People are so much more interesting that the stereotypes they inevitably get defined by because of their beliefs. And when you get past those flash points that only serve to divide, you begin to relate with people on a deeper and more authentic level which paves the way for some meaningful relationships to form. To me, this is intrinsically communal and holy—and perhaps the most significant impact Pub Theology has had on me."—Angela

WARNING

A word of caution should also be noted here. If you begin to travel this path of openness and inquiry, there are no guarantees. I cannot guarantee you that if you begin to analyze your faith more closely you will automatically grow in your faith. That could happen. It might not. Such analysis could also result in your deciding that it is no longer tenable for you. I'm OK with that. It may well be preferable to have no faith rather than an unreflective faith, or worse, a faith façade.

Note well: you will face resistance on this journey. You will be mis-understood as you venture out from beyond the safe enclaves of church and certainty. This will be threatening to some, and you'll be vilified and called various things. But you will also find yourself on a journey toward openness and wonder, and I hope, toward God.

It should also be noted that the path is not easy that begins to ques-tion long held certainties and that begins to analyze assumptions. There may be some feeling of being afloat at sea with no anchor. However, the easy path is not always the best path, and if you can find some travel partners, so much the better!

A CRUCIAL DIFFERENCE

So maybe you'll make a few friends, maybe you'll learn something new, but is all this really worth it given the risks? You might conclude, "Perhaps its better to just stay safe and operate in my present circles." I would state that there are bigger things on the table here. Things that matter deeply— not only for you and me, but for our world.

Philip Gulley articulates what's really at stake:

> "I grew up in the heart of the Cold War and as a small child quickly adopted the us vs. them mentality of my culture. In that world-view, the globe was neatly divided into friends and enemies. Our enemies, the communists, were not like us. They did not believe in the Christian God, did not value human life, and did not cherish freedom or acknowledge human potential. When I was a young adult, the Iron Curtain fell and with it many of the old animosities. In some instances our former enemies became our allies against our new enemies, the terrorists. These terrorists, I've been told, do not believe in the Christian God, do not value human life, and do not cherish freedom. Someday, if history is any guide, our current enemies will no longer be perceived as our foes and a new enemy will rise to take their place. Unless . . ."[6]

Unless we learn to respect each and every person. Unless we take seriously the call to engage one another in open and honest dialogue. Unless we begin to acknowledge that the increasing diversity of the spiritual landscape around us is not a threat, but a blessing. Unless we are willing to admit that we don't have all the answers. Unless we see that perhaps there are answers others have that we do not. Unless we realize

6. Gulley, *The Evolution of Faith*, 87.

that demonizing those who see the world differently is not the best way forward for our society and our world. Unless we Christians truly begin to own the biblical vision that each and every single person has been created by God.

My contention is that the way forward for my own faith involves moving from a place of preaching, to a place of listening. From a position of teaching to a position of learning. From a place of fear to a place of openness. From a place of certainty to a place of wonder. From a place of hostility to a place of love.

Thanks to these pub gatherings, my own faith journey going forward will necessarily include the insights of Muslims, Buddhists, atheists, and others. I ignore them to my own spiritual peril. I, for one, cannot simply dismiss others as having nothing to teach me about God. God is bigger than that. Life is more complex than that. And for me, both the largeness of God and the complexity of life are what make the journey a beautiful thing. We are all walking the path of being human. Can we stop bickering over who has the best or truest path, or whose mode of transportation is superior? At some point, isn't it worth trying to travel a bit together? We might just find we enjoy one another's company, and that, my friends, will make the world a better place. And who knows? Perhaps somewhere along the way, some genuine personal and spiritual transformation will take place. Who would have thought that sitting down over a beer could matter so much?

Recommended Reading

Caputo, John D. *On Religion*. London: Routledge, 2001.

Feiler, Bruce. *Where God Was Born: A Journey By Land to the Roots of Religion*. New York: Morrow, 2005.

Gulley, Philip. *The Evolution of Faith*. New York: HarperOne, 2011.

Hirschfield, Brad. *You Don't Have to Be Wrong for Me to Be Right: Finding Faith Without Fanaticism*. New York: Three Rivers Press, 2009.

Keller, Timothy. *The Reason for God: Belief in an Age of Skepticism*. New York: Dutton, 2009.

Küng, Hans. *Does God Exist?* New York: Vintage, 1981.

Lane, Christopher. *The Age of Doubt: Tracing the Roots of Our Religious Uncertainty*. New Haven: Yale University Press, 2011.

McLaren, Brian. *A Generous Orthodoxy*. Grand Rapids: Zondervan, 2004.

Selmanovic, Samir. *It's Really All About God: How Islam, Atheism and Judaism Made Me a Better Christian*. San Francisco: Jossey-Bass, 2011.

Stark, Thom. *The Human Faces of God: What Scripture Reveals When It Gets God Wrong (And Why Inerrancy Tries to Hide It)*. Eugene, OR: Wipf and Stock, 2010.

Suk, John. *Not Sure: A Pastor's Journey From Faith to Doubt*. Grand Rapids: Eerdmans, 2011.

Tickle, Phyllis. *The Great Emergence: How Christianity is Changing and Why*. Grand Rapids: Baker Books, 2008.

Permissions

"Happiness For the Non-Believer" by Derek Del Barrio. Used by permission of the author. http://www.reject.org.

"The Last Trial" from *The Orthodox Heretic and Other Impossible Tales*. © Copyright 2009 by Peter Rollins. Used by permission of Paraclete Press.

Bibliography

Caputo, John D. *The Weakness of God*. Bloomington: Indiana University Press, 2006.

————. *What Would Jesus Deconstruct?* Grand Rapids: Baker Academic, 2007.

Conder, Tim and Daniel Rhodes, *Free For All: Rediscovering the Bible in Community*. Grand Rapids: Baker, 2009.

Del Barrio, Derek. "Happiness For the Non-Believer". http://www.reject.org/religion.html#happiness.

Ellul, Jacques. *What I Believe*. Grand Rapids: Zondervan, 1989.

Fowler, James. *Stages of Faith: The Psychology of Human Development and the Quest for Meaning*. New York: HarperOne, 1995.

Howard-Brooks, Wes. *Becoming Children of God*. Eugene, OR: Wipf and Stock, 2003.

Gulley, Philip. *The Evolution of Faith*. New York: HarperOne, 2011.

Herzog, William. *Parables as Subversive Speech*. Louisville: Westminster/John Knox, 1994.

Jones, Tony. *The Church Is Flat: The Relational Ecclesiology of the Emerging Church Movement*. Minneapolis: JoPa Productions, 2011.

Knitter, Paul F. *Introducing Theologies of Religion*. Maryknoll, NY: Orbis, 2005.

London, Jack. *The Sea Wolf*. New York: Bantam, 1960.

McLaren, Brian. *A Generous Orthodoxy*. Grand Rapids: Zondervan, 2004.

Muesseldorfer, Franz G. "A Comprehensive History of Beer Brewing." http://media.wiley.com/product_data/excerpt/44/35273167/3527316744.pdf.

Rollins, Peter. *The Fidelity of Betrayal*. Brewster, MA: Paraclete, 2008.

————. *How (Not) to Speak of God*. Brewster, MA: Paraclete, 2009.

————. *The Orthodox Heretic, and Other Impossible Tales*. Brewster, MA: Paraclete, 2009.

Pagitt, Doug. *Preaching Re-Imagined*. Grand Rapids: Zondervan, 2005.

Stark, Thom. *Behold the Man: What the Bible Doesn't Say About the Divinity of Jesus*. Eugene, OR: Wipf and Stock, forthcoming.

Taylor, Barbara Brown. *Speaking of Sin*. Boston: Cowley, 2000.

Westphal, Merold. *Whose Community? Which Interpretation?: Philosophical Hermeneutics for the Church*. Grand Rapids: Baker Academic, 2009.

Wills, Gary. *Saint Augustine*. New York: Viking, 1999.

Wright, N. T. *Surprised by Hope: Rethinking Heaven, the Resurrection, and the Mission of the Church*. New York: HarperOne, 2008.